MICHEL FOUCAULT
Social Theory and Transgression

MICHEL FOUCAULT
Social Theory and Transgression

Charles C. Lemert
and Garth Gillan

1982
COLUMBIA UNIVERSITY PRESS
NEW YORK

Library of Congress Cataloging in Publication Data

Lemert, Charles C., 1937–
  Michel Foucault: social theory and
transgression.

  Bibliography: p.
  Includes index.
  1. Foucault, Michel. I. Gillan, Garth,
1939–   . II. Title.
B2430.F72L45   303.3′092′4   82-4276
ISBN 0-231-05190-5   AACR2
ISBN 0-231-05191-3 (pbk.)

Columbia University Press
New York   Guildford, Surrey

Clothbound editions of Columbia University Press books are Smyth-
sewn and printed on permanent and durable acid-free paper.

Contents

Preface   vii

1. *Background*/FOUCAULT'S FIELD   1

2. *Method*/HISTORICAL ARCHAEOLOGY   29

3. *Substance*/POWER-KNOWLEDGE AND DISCOURSE   57

4. *Problems*/LIMITS AND SOCIAL THEORY   93

Appendix: Concepts Used by Foucault   127

Notes   139

Foucault's Publications   153

Index   161

Preface

MICHEL FOUCAULT was born in 1926. He is widely read—in France, and abroad. He is Professor of the History of Systems of Thought at the Collège de France. He writes on such a wide range of topics that his readers include people interested in literature, philosophy, history, sociology, politics, psychiatry, medicine, linguistics, and semiotics. He is known to do most of his own research at the Bibliothèque Nationale in Paris. He is an elegant, though to some obscure, writer. He is, in his way, politically active. He is bald as well as brilliant and, because of this, he is an imposing figure.

This is about all we will say about Foucault, the personality. It is important to clear the air on this matter because, in our opinion, Foucault should not be read as an intellectual hero. To do so would be to obscure the critical questions that must be asked of him. Foucault, like anyone else worth reading, is valuable to us for the habits of mind he shatters and the visions of new work to which he points. What he intends and how he leads his life are irrelevant to these considerations. This book, therefore, is about what Foucault has written, not Foucault, the man.

But to turn from the man to the writings is merely to exchange one set of problems for another. Authors of books, like this one, on the writings of another, like Foucault, are tempted on several sides. Our temptations owe to a conflict of demands. There are, after all, important differences of interest on three sides. Our interests, those of readers, and those of the author written about are not the same. Readers want, among other things, guidance, clarity, and explanation. Otherwise, presumably, they would not bother with someone else's interpretations. This is their right, but this right is not absolute. The author whose work is under examination usually wants to be taken seriously on his own terms. Foucault is no exception. More than once he has objected to those who, in his opinion, have misread him. The interests of readers and authors examined are not perfectly reconcilable, especially when the former find the latter difficult and the latter take the intentional risk of being difficult for what they consider good purposes. Clarity and intellectual subtlety are not always equivalently attainable goals. This is not to say that readers should be excused for their frequent unwillingness to dig against someone else's subtlety or that authors should be forgiven when they use nuance to escape the demands of clarity.

Hence, the temptations of so-called secondary authors, those who write books like ours. We desire that our books be read but, just as much, that we not make fools of ourselves. Too much attention to readers' interests in clarity and we become fools for having destroyed whatever is legitimately subtle in our subject. Too much commitment to the subject's complexity and we become foolish enthusiasts. Neither type of fool deserves to be read.

We attempt, therefore, to guard against the extremes of temptation by a definite literary strategy. We distinguish a book's structure from its style, and assume that each level can bear different responsibilities. To the structural level we have assigned the task of caring for reader's interests in clarity and explanation; to style we give the difficult task of representing Foucault, fairly but critically, on his own terms. This book, therefore, structures the chapters around questions readers have asked or should have asked of Foucault. Within each chapter we try to present Foucault in a manner that demonstrates his probable response while maintaining sufficient critical distance to remind the reader that his questions are indeed fair and responsible.

QUESTIONS OF FOUCAULT.   There are at least four perfectly reasonable questions one should ask of Foucault's writings.

Where does he come from? A reader usually wants to know
something of a writer's intellectual background. This question
is particularly pertinent in Foucault's case. To many he appears
to come out of nowhere. This is partly due to his refusal to
name those with whom he argues, and partly to his method.
He does, however, have what we normally would call a background even if, in his objection to the idea of founding a
tradition of thought, he disguises it. Chapter 1, therefore,
explains why he cannot be understood as a Marxist, a structuralist, or a semiotician—these being the traditions into which
others want to insert him. We show, in this chapter, that
Foucault's background is more a matter of specific problems
to which he has been exposed by his teachers and contempor-
aries. Our view is that though he works with a definite
relationship to the *Annales* historians, Bachelard's history of
science, and to Nietzsche, he is more concerned with their
questions than their answers, Foucault's specific problems are
those of history, the knowledge of man, and language.

Why does he write like that? This is surely the first and perhaps
the most common question asked of Foucault. He has been
accused of willful obscurity. But this complaint runs counter
to the fact that, even when one cannot be sure what he is
saying, it is evident that he is saying it well. If Foucault creates
the impression of obscurity, it is for a reason. His reasons may
be arguable, but the difficulty of his prose is surely not because
he is a literary incompetent. Actually Foucault's literary style
is a direct consequence of his intellectual, especially historical,
method. Chapter 2, therefore, deals with Foucault's method,
but begins by explaining how his method is related to the
stylistic conventions which are most troubling to readers. In
discussing his method, we attempt furthermore, to disabuse
readers of the idea that his *Archaeology of Knowledge* is of special
importance. *Archaelogy of Knowledge* is not a methodological

statement, though it provides an acceptable but limited and abstract guide to that method. Our main argument, here and throughout the book, is that to understand what Foucault is trying to do one must read his specific historical studies. When this approach is taken, the reader has much less difficulty with his style because here one can actually see him at work in a definite way and appreciate what is at stake methodologically.

What is he getting at? This question should be asked with considered ambiguity. Foucault does not write in order to teach lessons, or promote a political or philosophical line. His is not a thinly veiled discourse behind which is found a message. Nonetheless, his writing is political in two ways. His historical studies seek to explain the conditions out of which have arisen specific social conflicts in our society. And he writes politically in that, at every point, he challenges tradition and works to pose new questions by means of new methods. Therefore, he is getting at something which is less a message than a series of problems.

Chapter 3 examines the substantive core of Foucault's theoretical position. Foucault refuses to work within any of the academic or literary specialties, narrowly and exclusively defined. Rather, he works across the disciplinary boundaries, combining history, philosophy, and politics. This involves the concept with which he is uniquely identified, power/knowledge, and the topic with respect to which he is so often misunderstood, discourse. After explaining the evolution of these basic concepts, chapter 3 analyzes the way in which they are played out in his historical studies and philosophical essays. We do not, however, trace the chronological evolution of Foucault's thought or mechanically proof text the various occurrences of Foucault's theory of power and knowledge. Rather, we have presented these discussions with reference to the working concepts by which Foucault concretely describes and analyzes power/knowledge. These are transgression, the body, and politics and death.

Where has he gone wrong? And why bother to read him? Though critical questions are posed throughout, chapter 4 explicitly presents the major problems in Foucault's work to date, and speculates, somewhat frankly, about his possible contributions to social theory. We have not attempted to cite or summarize all the secondary literature on Foucault. Rather our critique is immanent. It makes little sense to us to try to show that if he had done something else he might have avoided certain traps. Criticism, in this case, obliges one to take seriously what he has done, right or wrong, and then to ask, where does he come up short? It is easy to make mincemeat of someone like Foucault for having failed to do something else. To be sure, had he been a better Marxist, his class analysis would have been more obvious. Had he done traditional history, his facts would have conformed more to customary interpretations. Had he not so sternly rejected phenomenology, he might have presented a better solution to the problem of the subject. But since he is not a Marxist, a positivist, a phenomenologist, or anything else in particular, it hardly suffices to bring external evaluative standards to his work. It is more to the point, if more difficult, to take seriously what he has done in order to diagnose his errors.

Of course, intelligent criticism requires something with which that criticized can be compared. We have chosen to compare Foucault to a very broad intellectual field of work, but one to which he bears comparison. Thus, social theory, taken as the collection of intellectual activities which recognize the role of power in our knowledge of the social, is the field against which Foucault is measured. Given recent debates in social history, on the theory of the subject, and on the role of reason in revolution, we indicate where Foucault is limited. Then, using the same comparisons, we suggest where Foucault's most unique if yet to be realized contributions might lie.

STYLE.   It is well known that writings about someone sometimes take on the style of their subject. Often this happens because the interpreter is simply enamoured of the one interpreted. In these cases similarity of style is a not so silent tribute. There is, however, another reason to write in a manner comparable to one's subject. In some cases it is simply impossible to present without representing. To be sure, the line between mimicry and intelligent representation is easily breached. If readers occasionally think that we have lost sight of the distinction, we would hope they'd look closer, and judge us against our method. Foucault's writing is strange and unfamiliar. Justice cannot be done to whatever he has done if we were to rewrite him into some artificially "clear" style. Were style not so bound up with Foucault's method, it might have been possible to translate him. But it is, so we have not. Readers may find our appendix, *Concepts Used by Foucault,* a useful guide to problems involved in reading him, but even here we have not tried to translate his language into some other. Popularizations have their place, but not, we think, in the case of someone, like Foucault, who insists that thinking and writing must always be done against the limits of the normal. It is doubtful that a successful high school manual could be written for Joyce's *Ulysses.* Foucault is not as opaque as Joyce, but like Joyce his style and his thought are inseparable.

Of course, anyone who has seriously read *The Order of Things* could not unambiguously believe that representation straightforwardly expresses the truth of the represented. Some would want to say at this point that texts on another's texts are primary in their own right, and thus that representation is a literary impossibility. This claim, it seems to us, is extreme to the same degree as is its opposite: that secondary interpretations derive their validity solely from the exactness of their conformity to the original. Behind this debate over the independence or derivativeness of interpretations is once again the triumvirate with which this introduction began: interpreters, interpreted, and their readers. Interpreters cannot afford to distance themselves from either of the first two, and this fact affects their style and their method.

Our method, as interpreters and critics, has been to take up a position somewhere between Foucault and his readers. Of course these readers are not so anonymous as, so far, we have made it seem. Our best estimates of readers' attitudes toward Foucault are based on our reading of what others have written about him and our discussions with students and colleagues who are interested in him. These people, for us, are Foucault's readers, and they are largely, if not exclusively, social theorists. Not only does Foucault write across disciplinary boundaries, he is also read in this way.

In other words, Foucault's readers tend to be those who, to greater or lesser extents, acknowledge that no single intellectual specialization is sufficient to the task of explaining the social world. They are, it seems fair to assume, people who share Foucault's conviction that the disciplines are both insufficient and part of the problem of modern society.

Thus, the tactic of situating ourselves between Foucault and this kind of reader is justified on wider grounds than those of a certain style of presentation. The very fact that he is widely read and largely by an intellectually restless readership suggests something of Foucault's importance. And this has implications for the way in which he ought to be approached.

We live in an intellectual world from which, in a short span of time, a good number of heroes have passed. In the few years prior to the publication of this book, many social theorists of differing stripes have died or otherwise passed from the scene—Arendt, Althusser, Barthes, Gouldner, Marcuse, Poulantzas, Parsons, Sartre. While others remain and, no doubt, younger people are seeking these vacated statuses, the deaths cannot help but make us rethink the very idea of an intellectual hero. This is an especially sobering thought when we compare the present situation with the wild enthusiasm of the immediately preceeding period. It was, after all, but a decade ago that the human sciences celebrated what turned out to be a short-lived moment of theoretical innovation. Critical theory, phenomenology, semiotics, ethnomethodology, structuralism were just the more fashionable of many experiments and programs for the renewal of modern social thought. Stars were born, but the renewal of the sciences of man did not take place.

Foucault and many of his readers were part of this now passed inebriating period. It is natural in the face of failures of renewal and the loss of other stars for many to turn to those, like Foucault, who remain. This is exactly the wrong way to approach Foucault, or anyone else.

The times no longer demand heroes and programs, but careful and specific work, theoretical and empirical. The new mood is appropriately sober. Social theorists are increasingly interested in concrete studies and decreasingly impressed by abstract proposals for paradigmatic rehabilitation. Just as much a growing number are willing to work at the intellectual margins of the university disciplines and departments which pay their salaries. If this is not the dominant mood in the academic human sciences, it is prominent. And it is to these readers, we think, that Foucault promises the most.

Foucault is most interesting when he is working on specific historical, literary, or philosophical problems. And he is interesting for two reasons above all. First, his empirical studies are theoretically sophisticated. His critique of the disciplines, his exposé of anthropologism, his gradual development of a theory of power, his implicit theories of intellectuals and ideology, his philosophy of science, among other things, are each presented in concrete terms and against specific problems in literary theory, social history, and philosophy. Second, he works with scant regard for convention. If this disregard appears, on occasion, to be trendy, it remains that his method is one that transgresses traditional rules. These two attributes combined mean that he continues to do social history and social theory while challenging both. This seems to us to be the proper model for work in a time such as ours. Further, it requires us to read him, and others, in a certain way. Not as a hero, but as a worker; not for a general theory of society or Man, but for concrete investigations of hospitals, prisons, academies, confessionals, and bedrooms. This means that he should be read on his own terms. This is what we have tried to do.

ACKNOWLEDGMENTS.   William Schwartz was the principal research assistant on the project. He gathered, from various parts, many sometimes obscure texts, then ordered them for us. The Humanities and Social Science librarians at Morris Library, Southern Illinois University at Carbondale, were wonderfully supportive. They acquired for our use many texts not in our private collections. We would like especially to thank the Humanities librarian, Alan Cohn, for his special attention to our project. Even as the manuscript goes to press he continues to send references our way. The manuscript was typed by Kim Grandys and Mary McTaggart. Robin Pressman and Mizan Miah helped in other ways to prepare the manuscript. Jerry Gaston generously supported the project. Robert K. Merton kindly helped Lemert gain an appointment as Visiting Scholar at Columbia University, during which visit, he, Lemert, was able to uncover needed materials and write. John Moore and Charles Webel gave excellent editorial advice. None of these people is guilty of anything pertinent to this book except help, kindness, and generosity.

Finally, we would like to thank especially our children for their long suffering through snacks unprovided, noses unwiped, struggles unadjudicated, and other tribulations we ignored but for dim noises in the background. More than once we slighted our respective child care duties for long phone conversations. As for our wives, as usual they simply understood. Somewhere in all this we also found time and space to think.

Charles Lemert
Middletown, Connecticut

Garth Gillan
Cobden, Illinois

MICHEL FOUCAULT
Social Theory and Transgression

1. Background / FOUCAULT'S FIELD

WHAT IS Michel Foucault? Marxist? Structuralist? Semiotician? He uses Marx's terms: class, political economy, commodity, capital, labor power, struggle. Yet, if this is Marxism, its affiliation is unclear. The structuralist interest in the universal forms of culture is there in Foucault's talk of "order in its primary state" and his attempt to "uncover the deepest strata of Western culture."[1] Yet, again and again, he renounces his structuralism. A semiotician's hand is surely at work in his studies of General Grammar in *The Order of Things* and of the relation between signs and symptoms in *Birth of the Clinic*.[2] Yet, Foucault is obviously much more than a semiotician.

Marxist, structuralist, semiotician. These labels are those of his readers, not his. When, reading Foucault, we encounter the new and the strange in his writing, we do what readers must do. We use what we know, or think we know, to naturalize the new. We read from the familiar to the strange. Since Foucault is a French intellectual writing after the existentialist period, he must be, we assume, Marxist, structuralist, or semiotician. What else, after all, is there in this period in France? Such an assumption, rigidly employed, only creates problems. Such a reading strategy may serve us well in some cases, but it fails with Foucault. Some authors fit categories. Foucault does not.

Foucault's writings constantly push us from the familiar to

the strange. The reader is aware of an unyielding limit. The limit enclosing our familiar stock of knowledge does not always expand as we read. We cannot trade on a knowledge of Marxism, structuralism, semiotics. We are obliged to transgress, to go beyond what we know, to let ourselves fall into the strangeness of his language and thought, and to wonder if what we are reading has any worth at all.

Hence, there are rules in reading Foucault. Don't make him something else. Learn to live with what he is. Make your judgments after reading a great deal. Yes, of course, much can be gained from tendentious readings: a sociology of punishment in *Discipline and Punish*, an epistemology of the human sciences in *The Order of Things*, a philosophical deconstruction of power theory in *The History of Sexuality*, Vol. I., a metaphilosophy of historical knowledge in *Archaeology of Knowledge*, a theory of the political intellectual in "Truth and Power,"[3] literary studies of Bataille, Blanchot, Flaubert, Roussel, Nietzsche in *Language, Counter-memory, and Practice*.[4] Much stands on its own and can be absorbed into projects external to Foucault. But whoever wants to understand Foucault should not make him something he is not. Take him on his own, difficult terms.

One of the reasons why Foucault pushes us over the boundary of the familiar is that he is Parisian. Parisian intellectuals work in a complex, rapidly changing field of intellectual forces.[5] Ideas come and go. Intellectual stars rise and fall, sometimes within a matter of weeks. No other intellectual place in the modern world is quite comparable to Paris. It is an epicenter in which most of the force of the world's francophone culture and learning is concentrated. As a result, authors and their ideas must compete for a position in this field. Few hold their own for very long. Writers must meet the needs of a demanding and fickle literary public. Intellectuals are under constant observation on the pages of *Le Monde* or the *Nouvel Observateur*, on the screens of French television, on the platforms of the Collège de France, Beaubourg, or FNAC. Since literary acceptance is a sign of intellectual worth, there is little hiding from *tout Paris.* Once a writer exposes himself to such a public, all its force storms over him. Thus, in order to avoid embarrassment, Parisian intellectuals are under tremendous pressure to seek refuge in the strange, the new. This is why so much French literature and human science is underglossed and overcoded.[6] Stylistic and intellectual inventiveness function to protect the author's precarious position in an intemperate intellectual climate. Foreign readers, especially Americans, experience this first hand. We discover Merleau-Ponty, Sartre, Lévi-Strauss, Althusser, Gurvitch, Barthes, Derrida, Kristeva, Poulantzas, Henri-Lévy, then rush to Paris to visit these monuments but find only the rubble. The storm has passed us by. The stars are either gone, or have moved on into an even stranger lexical galaxy. No one in Paris wants to talk about them. The French find our interest in their monuments quaint.

Foucault is a part of this field. Though he has not yet lost his literary place in Paris, his writing bears the marks of its pressures. It is strange, perhaps, to the degree that it has held its own for twenty years, since the publication in 1961 of his first major book, *Histoire de la folie.*[7]

There is, however, another more fundamental explanation of Foucault's strangeness. He has turned the complex conditions of the Parisian intellectual into a positive method. Foucault is not frivolously idiosyncratic. Whatever may be the final judgment on his work, he intends to write and work as he does. His social theory explicitly employs the transgression of familiar limits.

FOUCAULT, THE EVENT.   To call Foucault an event is not to celebrate him, or to make of him more than he is. It is to consider him on his own terms. Foucault rejects *histoire événementielle,* the traditional history of great events (wars, treaties, diplomatic accords, and so forth). He proposes instead a history which neutralizes the usual understanding of historical events. In the place of great events Foucault takes seriously the ignoble in history: forgotten novels, a homicide's memoire, an hermaphrodite's story, a single tableau from the oeuvre of Magritte.[8] An event is not measured by its inherent meaning or importance, but externally by its place in a field of social forces. An event is a locus of chance reversal. "We must accept the introduction of chance as a category in the production of events."[9] Foucault's event is not the causal origin of change, but the specific, discontinuous moment when a transformation is evident. Therefore, to speak of Foucault, the event, is not to ask what great meanings, private intentions, or social totalities he represents. It is to set aside the usual questions of his background, his tradition, his sources, his influences, his line of continuity, his significance, his deeper meaning. It is, simply, to locate his writing where it is different and specific with respect to "its external conditions of existence."[10]

Foucault is an event in respect to which one can see the two major reversals in recent French thought. He was not their cause. Nor does he purely represent them. In fact, in both instances, Foucault is clearly eccentric to these transformations. Nonetheless, in his difference from the fields of which he has been a part, one can see both the concreteness of his position and the general features of the field of forces which, externally, conditioned that position.

The first transformation was the structuralist movement. Foucault's *Madness and Civilization* (1961) appeared in the midst of the structuralist controversy. The high water mark of structuralism was, roughly, between 1955 (Lévi-Strauss' *Tristes tropiques*) and the mid-60s (Althusser's *For Marx*, 1966; Griemas' *Semantique structurale*, 1966; Poulantzas' *Political Power and Social Classes*, 1968).[11] Though structuralism was itself a many sided movement and by no means the only intellectual activity of merit at the time, it posed questions which separated it decisively from post-World War Two existentialism and phenomenology. Is history, in fact, reducible to actions of the historical subject? Does not language explain the human mind better than consciousness? How can the study of the human be scientific? Obviously, the questions and their answers overlapped. But, in the range of activities between Lévi-Strauss' use of Jakobson's linguistics in a critique of historicism and Althusser's rediscovery of the scientific Marx against Marxian humanism, structuralism transformed French thought. The historical subject, the crypto-metaphysics of consciousness, and the privileging of hermeneutics in the human sciences were all, abruptly, called into doubt. In their place were issues of a wholly different nature. Is not the subject a product of social forces? Cannot consciousness be read from language? Can there not be a formal or, at least, universalizing science of man without interpretation? In short, structuralism asked: what is history? what is language? what is knowledge of the human? Against historicism, it deployed Saussure's synchrony. Against phenomenology, it privileged language (*la langue*) as such over the speaking subject. Against hermeneutics, it returned to the analysis of form and the general.

Foucault was an event in this controversy. He asked the same questions. But, before the decade was over, he explicitly rejected structuralism.[12] The rejection was necessary because in the books of this period—*Madness and Civilization, The Order of Things*, and *Archaeology of Knowledge*—he worked in the same intellectual region as did structuralism, though without being a structuralist.

The second transformation in recent French thinking occurred within structuralism, and was less turbulent. It appeared to be an adjustment from within, but may turn out to have been its ending. Between Derrida's three books in 1967 (*Speech and Phenomena, Writing and Difference, Of Grammatology*) and Deleuze and Guattari's *Anti-Oedipus: Capitalism and Schizophrenia* (1972) and Bourdieu's *Outline of a Theory of Practice* (1973),[13] structuralism was confronted at its weakest points: the vestiges of humanism and phonocentrism in Saussure and Lévi-Strauss, its inability to provide a political account of historical cultures, its objectivism, and, especially, its overlooking of the desiring, practicing social subject. Here the break was not as clean as the earlier one with existentialism. The so-called post-structuralist movement took for granted structuralism's rejection of meta-physics, its interest in language and literature, and its refusal to reduce man to the ideal subject. But, benefiting in part from a Lacanian revival[14] as well as from independent readings of Freud, Nietzsche, and Marx (among others), post-structuralism resuscitated the questions of subjectivity, historical action, and practice. The subject was not the old transcendental subjectivity of consciousness, but of desire mediated through language and literature. Historical action was no longer human engagement, but the politics of writing and madness. Practice was not the expression of intentions, but strategies determined by the conjunction of social forces and human desire.[15] It is not surprising that this later transformation is punctuated by the year of revolution, 1968. Thereafter, it was no longer plausible to think abstractly of frozen synchronies, of ahistorical man, of social structures (linguistic included) as unilateral determinants of social action, of subjects without desires or the threat of death. If structuralism put an end to existentialism's crypto-liberalism, then post-structuralism drew the line on structur-alism's latent abstractionism and apoliticism.

Foucault no less was an event in this second reversal. In *Discourse on Language*, his inaugaural address in 1970 at the Collège de France, he began to clarify the role of critique in his historical studies.[16] Thereafter, in *Discipline and Punish* (1975) and *History of Sexuality* (1976) he was careful to expunge all traces of a unidirectional deterministic theory of power. Power was no longer from above, the excluding action of structures on individuals. It was, equally, an immanent process, tied closely to knowledge and discourse, which operates as a technique on all levels of society.[17] The desiring individual was both a product and producer of sexuality. The political intel-lectual was not the judge speaking to and on behalf of the masses, but the concrete intellectual engaged in regional stud-ies.[18] We should be careful not to initiate a two-Foucault debate. There is no early and late Foucault in the sense that suddenly, after 1970, he discovered the ubiquity of power and the politics of truth. Nietzsche, Bataille, Artaud, and Freud were there from the beginning.[19] If Foucault was not changed, he was at least marked by the events of 1968.

This is to say that Foucault the event is both structuralist, and post-structuralist, yet neither. He is an occurrence in these transformations, yet he retains his own specificity. Just as these two reversals are greater than Foucault, so Foucault is in excess of them. These transformations posed questions of history, of language, of knowledge, and ultimately, of politics. Foucault was and is an event in his time. But, just as much, he and these forces are selectively members of a series of events, series which preceded structuralism and surely will outlive post-structuralism.

We cannot, therefore, talk of Foucault's background, but of his place, as an event, in series which act as intellectual forces. The question of history, for Foucault, is a question put by Marx, Nietzsche, and the *Annales* historians. The question of knowledge, for him, is posed in large part by Bachelard and Canguilhem, among others. The question of language is posed by Bataille, Blanchot, Artaud, Nietzsche, and Freud. To read Foucault is to come invariably to series of names such as these. The series vary and overlap. They mark not his sources but the dispersed classes of events of which he is a proper member.

If we begin with familiar designations—Marxist, structuralist, semiotician—and then dismiss them, it is only to move into the strangeness of Foucault's concreteness. Concrete events, in their particularity, are necessarily less familiar than the labels by which we try to organize them. Of course Foucault is marked by Marxism, structuralism, and semiotics, but his specificity is in their overlapping and their excess, in his way of responding to questions of history, knowledge, and language.

HISTORY.   Were we to rely on the familiar, Foucault could appear to be very Marxist. He clearly identifies Marx as a crucial turning point in historical method.[20] It was Marx who led the way to a positive explanatory method, liberated from moral denunciation.[21] In *Discipline and Punish* Foucault explicitly cites Marx's analysis of constant and variable capital in *Capital*, Vol. 1, in order to explain the modern prison as an instrument of disciplining power. "In fact, the two processes— the accumulation of men and the accumulation of capital— cannot be separated; it would not have been possible to solve the problem of the accumulation of men without the growth of an apparatus of production capable of both sustaining them and using them; conversely the techniques that made the cumulative multiplicity of men useful accelerated the accumulation of capital."[22] This is one of his most explicit references to Marx's method, but there are others. The confinement of the mad in asylums, in *Madness and Civilization*, and of the poor in the teaching clinic, in *Birth of the Clinic*, are both related to a theory of productive relationships, the creation of surplus labour and a political economy of poverty . The asylum was differentiated from other forms of confinement at the point at which "poverty became an economic phenomenon."[23] Perforce the mad were, by the nineteenth century, segregated from the poor and the unproductive idle. The mad required special treatment because they were more irreducibly unproductive members of the population. Hence, in part, the modern asylum; hence also, the beginnings of modern corrective psychology. Likewise, at the dawn of the liberal age the teaching hospital was born, in part, of the use value of the bodies of the poor.

These, then, were the terms of the contract by which rich and poor participated in the organization of clinical experience. In a regime of economic freedom, the hospital had found a way of interesting the rich; the clinic constitutes the progressive reversal of the other contractual part; it is the *interest* paid by the poor on the capital that the rich have consented to invest in the hospital. . . . The doctor's gaze is a very small saving in the calculated exchanges of a liberal world.[24]

And, no less, in *The History of Sexuality* the social mechanisms for the discipline and regulation of sexuality were bound to a political economy requiring bodies for labor power. "The adjustment of the accumulation of men to that of capital, the joining of the growth of human groups to the expansion of productive forces and the differential allocation of profit, were made possible in part by the exercise of bio-power in its many forms and modes of application."[25] And, more generally, one constantly senses an affinity with Marx in Foucault's persistent critique of the nineteenth century, a critique which is most devastatingly presented in the famous announcement in *The Order of Things* of the death of liberal Man. Foucault's history appears very Marxist—in its vocabulary, as in its method.

Nonetheless, Foucault keeps his distance from Marxism.

But there is also on my part a sort of game about this. I often quote concepts, texts, and phrases from Marx, but without feeling obliged to add the authenticating label of a footnote and a laudatory phrase to accompany the quotation. Provided you do that, you're regarded as someone who knows and reveres Marx and will be suitably honoured in (so-called) Marxist journals. But I quote Marx without saying I am, without quotation marks, and because people are unable to recognize Marx's texts I am considered to be someone who doesn't quote Marx. Does a physicist feel it necessary to quote Newton and Einstein when he writes a work of physics?. . . . It is impossible at the present time to write history without using a whole series of concepts directly or indirectly related to Marx's thought and situating oneself within a horizon of thought which has been defined and described by Marx. One might even wonder what difference there could ultimately be between being a historian and being Marxist.[26]

Foucault could not more closely identify himself with Marx. Nor could he more clearly and perversely distance himself from contemporary French Marxism. This is typical of Foucault's method. Neither Marxist nor anti-Marxist, yet both. Hence, he attacks communistology and economism.[27] In fact, the most fundamental revision of his thought, the emergence of the concept power-knowledge in *Discipline and Punish*, bespeaks, in its name, a critique of Marxist economism and traditional class analysis. Power, as power-knowledge, is not the domination of the ruling classes.

Power comes from below; that is, there is no binary and all-encompassing opposition between rulers and ruled and the root of power relations, . . . One must suppose rather that the manifold relationships of force that take shape and come into play in the machinery of production, in families, limited groups, and institutions, are the basis for wide-ranging effects of cleavage that run through the social body as a whole."[28]

Of course, this was necessarily the discovery of an essential conviction throughout his work. "To state the case very simply: psychiatric internment, the psychological normalization of individuals, and penal institutions have, undoubtedly, a rather limited importance, if one only looks for their economic significance. However, in the general working of the machinery of power, they are, without a doubt, essential."[29]

Foucault is both Marxist and more than Marxist. This is why it is futile to talk of his sources. Foucault does not go back to a tradition, but works with the raw material of present, vital discursive events. Foucault writes not in the tradition of Marx, but with an excess left over after Marx, an excess made available by other forces in Foucault's intellectual field. Thus, Foucault's confrontation with history derives, in part, from that which is unthought[30] and unthinkable in Marxism and, in part, the unthought in two French historical traditions: *Annales* social history and Bachelardian history of science.

Historical method, for Foucault, is caught in the space between two ideas: history of the long term and discontinuity. The former is best known, in contemporary French thought, in Fernand Braudel's *la longue durée*; the latter in Louis Althusser's *coupure épistemologique*.[31] Both have antecedents: Marc Bloch and Lucien Febvre in Braudel's case, and Gaston Bachelard and Georges Canguilhem in Althusser's. Stable structures and discontinuities, history of the long term and the history of ruptures meet in Foucault. Meeting, they form a new set of questions for history.[32] He challenges, in particular, the concepts causality and continuity in traditional history. Behind both is the idealistic axiom of a meaningful history of events originating in a transcendental subject. In short, Foucault, working between *Annales* and Bachelard, performs a materialist critique of metaphysical history, of histories which assume a causal force between great men, great civilizations, or great events or, alternatively, assume a meaningful continuity founded in a transcendental Logos. Thus, Foucault sees history as "that which transforms *documents* into *monuments*."[33] The historian's document is not to be interpreted for the secrets of human intentions, but transformed into an inert monumental text to be related to other texts. The historian does not decipher, he materially juxtaposes textual monuments.

Foucault's method, therefore, owes much to the *Annales'* critique of *histoire événementielle*. Great human events are studied only in the larger context of long enduring material and economic structures. Braudel's *The Mediterranean*,[34] for example, is in three parts: "The Role of the Environment," a study of mountains, plains, rivers, sea routes, and climate; "Collective Destinies," an economic history of the Mediterranean region; and, only thereafter, "Events, Politics, and People." Social and political events are juxtaposed to the long durations of material and economic structures. History does not move along a linear path of human action. The human is conditioned by a material world. Just as pertinent is Braudel's method. *The Mediterranean* is, quite literally, a monumental study performed in all the major archives of Europe. Census counts, shipping manifests, ancient maps, agricultural reports, and other documents (primary and secondary) are taken up, cut into pieces, arranged into series. A map is in a series with census data, accounts of sheepherding, facts of climate. Migration is not, simply, a way of life but events occurring within long-term structures reconstructed from documents. Causality, in history, is not from human event to human event, but at the conjuncture of material, economic, and social forces. History does not run through time. The time of events is in the time of duration. Ultimately, time is spatialized.

The *Annales* method has left its traces on Foucault. Discursive practices are related to their discursive fields in *Archaeology of Knowledge*. General Grammar, an event in the knowledge of logic and language, is related to the tabular episteme of the Classical Age in *The Order of Things*. The practice of confinement, in *Madness and Civilization* and *Discipline and Punish*, is explained, in part, by the economic imperatives of early capitalism. In *Birth of the Clinic* the observation of the body is related to transformations in the structures of the Liberal Age at the beginning of the nineteenth century. Structure explains human events. But Foucault's structures are not static. He does not replace temporal with spatial analysis. Archaeology "does not try to freeze time and to substitute for its flux of events correlations that outline a motionless figure."[35] Rather he rejects a cryptometaphysics of human time. He allows all the many layers of social formation to have their own times. Hence, there can be repetition, return, and discontinuity, just as much as continuity. He, therefore, speaks not of social change, but of transformation.[36] History is not a question of progress, but rearrangements in the relations among the multiple forces— material, economic, social—that comprise a social formation.

Quite clearly, the *Annales'* method works in the unthought of Marxism. While it shares with Marxism a critique of liberal, progressive history, it has pushed beyond the study of economic structures to the even longer term material structures of climate and geography. To the same extent, Foucault has entered the great silence of *Annales* historiography. Having begun as a critique of positivist history of great events, the later *Annales* historians took on their own positivism. Ladurie, for example, embarrassingly, but necessarily, came to praise, without criticism, computerized quantitative history. But he does so in an essay published eventually along side an acknowledgement of the weak point in *Annales* history, the event.[37] Having rejected the positivism of great events, the *Annales* tradition has provided very little theory or analysis of the specific events in which transformations occur. "Present-day historiography, with its preference for the quantifiable, the statistical and the structural, has been obliged to suppress in order to survive, which is a pity. In the last few decades it has virtually condemned to death the narrative history of events and the individual biography."[38]

The specific discontinuous event is the *Annales'* unthought. Foucault crosses this embarrassing limit. The contradiction between stable structures and ruptures is only apparent. Bachelard, Canguilhem, Serres, Guerolt, and Althusser document the place of the discontinuous event. "One of the most essential features of the new history is probably this displacement of the discontinuous: its transference from the obstacle to the work itself: its integration into the discourse of the historian, where it no longer plays the role of an external condition that must be reduced but that of a working concept."[39] Foucault's history, therefore, is ordered around events in which the forces of history transform and reverse themselves: the first modern novel, the first observation of patients' bodies, the day on which the insane were liberated from Bicêtre, the disappearance of the Ship of Fools, the transformation of the spectacle of scaffold torture. If long-term structures reduce the unwarranted privilege of the human in history, the event as rupture prevents structures from emerging as unidirectional determinants of human action.

Foucault's ironic relationship to Althusser illustrates both his use of this Bachelardian idea and his transgression of it. Beyond the principles of discontinuity and rupture, both Foucault and Althusser relate history to a theory of discourse, both are engaged in the reconstruction of structural effects, and both work at the limits between the visible and the invisible, between innocence and guilt. But they disagree over the epistemological break in Marx. Althusser puts Marx at the center. For Althusser the epistemological break in political economy and historical method in the nineteenth century occur in the middle of Marx, 1845. For Foucault, Marx shares the economic epistemology of Ricardo.[40] Marx's break is limited to the theory of history and politics. Foucault cuts Marx into pieces, but the segments cannot be arranged linearly in time. For Foucault, Marx is not the originating author, the primitive source of an event in the history of knowledge. Rather Marx himself is dissected by the forces of his episteme: his economics remain liberal political economy, his theory of history and politics is a rupture with this past. In other words, while Althusser periodizes history and totalizes Marx, Foucault reads Marx as an event in the midst of independent layers of knowledge. Economic knowledge has its own time: history and politics have theirs. This is consistent with Foucault's general theory of transformation. Discontinuity is not a general concept, but a working tool. Discontinuities can only be analyzed concretely with respect to a field of events to which they belong and which they sometimes reverse. Foucault contests all formalizations in history: totalization, periodization, ahistorical structures. In this respect, Foucault is closer to Braudel, for whom climate, the land and the sea, economic systems, and politics each had its own time. In this sense Foucault is not the historian of discontinuities, but an historian of concrete events in concrete domains.

What is Foucault's history? With Marx, Braudel, and Bachelard, he rejects traditional history's idealism, positivism, and linearity. But Foucault is not, simply, a Marxist, a member of the *Annales* school, and pupil of Althusser. Rather he works in a space created by all three. He speaks where they are silent, as they speak to one another's silences. History crosses the limit between the said and the unsaid in order to reestablish yet other limits to be transgressed.

KNOWLEDGE.   Foucault, the historian, is above all an historian of knowledge. This is obvious in *The Order of Things* and *Archaeology of Knowledge*. *Birth of the Clinic*, too, is an history of the rise of medical knowledge. *History of Sexuality* is the introduction to a multi-volume study, *La Volonté de savoir*, the will to know. Even those studies that seem less concerned with knowledge, *Madness and Civilization* and *Discipline and Punish*, are in their own ways analyses of knowledge's relationship to social control. Foucault is an historian of knowledge. However, the category is too restricting. It designates merely his difference from other histories. Though he works with and against *Annales'* history, Foucault slights material structures. He does materialist studies of the ideal. Likewise, though he works in relation to Bachelardian history of science, Foucault is not, strictly speaking, an historian of science. He has little to say of the physical sciences with which Bachelard was preoccupied. Where he treats the biological sciences, as did Canguilhem, he does so with respect to the general question of knowledge. And he has little of Althusser's interest in using Bachelard to revive historical materialism as a science. As with his history, Foucault's history of knowledge is situated perversely in a space unoccupied by those from whom he has learned. "What archaeology tries to describe is not the specific structure of sciences, but the very different domain of *knowledge*."[41]

Nonetheless, Foucault's interest in knowledge is, in crucial respects, Bachelardian. Discontinuity, rupture, displacement, dispersion, problematic, epistemological obstacle, epistemological pluralism, the history of error, the critique of continuous history—these are fundamental concepts of Bachelard and his successor Canguilhem.[42] They are, it goes without saying, also basic to Foucault. More basic yet is that Foucault, like Bachelard, overcomes continuous history, in part, by writing a history of truth from the point of view of errors. For Bachelard the famous epistemological couples—philosophy/science, realism/rationalism, truth/error—are not dualities but poles. They are not choices, but givens. Science has its philosophical dimensions; philosophy is informed by science. Realism and rationalism are not, simply, mutually exclusive philosophical perspectives, but necessary dimensions of an epistemological profile.[43] History must not close itself within a system of truths, but must open itself to moments of error in which a no is said to the past, and the new initiated. From his early studies of science, *Le Nouvel Esprit scientifique* (1934) and *La Formation de l'esprit scientifique* (1938), through his explicit epistemological statement in the *Philosophy of No* (1940) to his development of this position in later works, such as *La Rationalisme appliqué* (1949) and *Le Materialisme rationnel* (1953), Bachelard worked and reworked a pluralistic philosophy of scientific knowledge. Unlike Thomas Kuhn's crypto-evolutionism,[44] Bachelard's discontinuous history insists on a constant contestation between the old and the new. Even the radically rationalist relativism of modern physics, Bachelard's foremost interest and model, has to contend with the residues of positivist and substantialist realism. "What is most of all striking is that the alleged unity of science never corresponds to a stable state."[45] Epistemology is the history of epistemologies, each of which is always present, in some form and to some degree, and each of which has its own history for the concrete scientist who affirms the new by saying no to the old. But, for Bachelard, the rejected concept remains in the scientist's epistemological profile. "The diagram of the atom proposed by Bohr a quarter of a century ago has . . . acted as a good image: there is nothing left of it. But it has suggested 'no' often enough so that it keeps its indispensable role as initiatory pedagogy. These 'no's' are happily coordinated; they are the real constituents of contemporary microphysics."[46]

For Foucault, similarly, knowledge is plural. Discontinuities in the history of knowledge do not cut off the old from the new. Concrete knowledges have their own times that overlap. Science is never pure. It is always ideological, thus filled with errors. But the correction of error does not free it from ideology.[47] And historical knowledge is not a simple struggle between realism and rationalism, between the empirical and the conceptual. Knowledge is that which is produced in the tension between these poles. Foucault criticizes the history of ideas no less than the history of events, while attempting, in his way, to do both. And, most obviously, Foucault writes his histories of knowledge with constant reference to error and failure: the collapse of the distinction between reason and unreason in *Madness and Civilization*, the error of bodily observations without an adequate theory of tissual systems in *Birth of the Clinic*, the error in the myth of penitential reform in *Discipline and Punish*, the error of the repressive hypothesis in *The History of Sexuality*, and so forth.

At the same time, Bachelardian history of science forms a limit beyond which Foucault works. In *Archaeology of Knowledge* Foucault explicitly defines his project of study with respect to that which was ignored by other historians of science.[48] Beginning with the Bachelardian idea that the sciences, broadly defined, have irregular, heterogenous, and dispersed times,[49] Foucault describes four separate thresholds through which a science may pass. The threshold of positivity is met when a type of discourse takes on its own individuality, though it may lack norms of validity, formal standards of truth, or axioms. The threshold of epistemologization is crossed when attempts, sometimes unsuccessful, are made to establish a coherent, valid, and verified body of knowledge. The threshold of scientificity is traversed when a body of knowledge determines formal criteria that are employed as laws for the construction of propositions. The threshold of formalization is crossed when, within the science, formal axioms are taken as the legitimate and self-evident starting points for knowledge.

At the three intervening thresholds, Foucault locates three types of history of science: one, the history of mathematics, at the threshold of formalization; two, the history of natural and physical sciences between epistemologization and scientificity, which was the area within which Canguilhem and Bachelard, respectively, worked; and three, Foucault's archaeological history, which is at the threshold of epistemologization, the point at which a body of knowledge begins to employ a coherent and independent discourse. These are not exclusive domains. Some sciences retain primitive metaphors alongside formal axioms.[50] But, Foucault goes beyond Bachelard by studying sciences at a more elementary threshold, at the point when their discourse is epistemologized, when they became knowledges, *connaissances*. Hence, his interest in the early human sciences, in the beginnings of clinical medicine and of psychopathology, in early penology. In short, Foucault studies sciences in which the margin between error and truth is most fragile, those most infested with ideology.

This is not, for Foucault, simply a programmatic departure from the example of his teachers. His work opens into an area in which Bachelard was largely silent. By radicalizing the history of error, Foucault takes the unthought in science as his primary object. The history of science "tries to restore what eluded [scientific] consciousness: the influences that affected it, the implicit philosophies that were subjacent to it, the unformulated thematics, the unseen obstacles; it describes the unconscious of science. This unconscious is always the negative side of science—that which resists it, deflects it, or disturbs it. What I would like to do, however, is to reveal a positive unconscious of knowledge: a level that eludes the consciousness of the scientist and yet is part of scientific discourse."[51] This is both Bachelard, and more Bachelard.

Foucault's study of the human sciences is, theoretically, an investigation of those sciences in which the human examines itself. Knowledge of Man, by men, is more than error filled. It is inherently contradictory. It is simultaneously the most intimate and the most impossible of knowledges. In sociology, this problem is recognized vaguely in the debates over the objectivity of social studies. For Foucault, this is a general philosophic question which he discusses at length at the end of *The Order of Things*. The human sciences came to be in the nineteenth century by the invention of Man. Man became the object of thought by being made the principal subject of his history. Knowledge of the human required, contradictorily, the transcendence of the human. Man can only think himself by, simultaneously, recognizing himself in going beyond himself. Critical thought and Man's self knowledge are coterminous. Since Kant, the question of man entailed the critique of man's knowledge and the recognition of its limits. Knowledge cannot rely on the Cartesian identity between Man's thought and his being. Rather, the nineteenth-century human sciences employed the transcendental Man, the universal Subject, with respect to which human thought could think the human.

It is well known, however, that Foucault is critical of this solution. The nineteenth century's homocentrism is at best an unacknowledged metaphysics. It placed Man at the center of thought and of historical being. It shared, thereby, a metaphysical interest in controlled knowledge. Man was liberated only superficially. In the guise of humanism, nineteenth-century thought secretly controlled thought by subjugating it to a transcendental ideal. Hence, Foucault's famous Nietzschean announcement of the death of man. The human, for Foucault, can only think itself by investigating without annulling the limits of the human. Knowledge of the human is decentered, at the margin between truth and error, innocence and guilt, the thought and the unthought.

Man has not been able to describe himself as a configuration in the *episteme* without thought at the same time discovering, both in itself and outside itself, at its borders yet also in its very warp and woof, an element of darkness, an apparently inert density in which it is embedded, an unthought which it contains entirely, yet in which it is also caught. The unthought (whatever name we give it) is not lodged in man like a shrivelled-up nature or a stratified history; it is, in relation to man, the Other; the Other that is not only a brother but a twin, born not of man, nor in man, but beside him and at the same time, in an identifical newness, in an unavoidable duality.[52]

It is clear, now, how Foucault's interest in knowledge of the human is, fundamentally, an interest in knowledge and power. His work is a critical social theory, in a post-Kantian sense. He studies, above all else, the birth of those knowledges which in the form of liberal humanism were actually technologies in a political economy of controlled labor. He investigates, with an obvious critical purpose, those disciplines, born at the same time as the industrialization of Europe, which functioned behind their enlightened, reformist exteriors to control human behavior: penology, psychology, clinical medicine, the sciences of life. Discipline is a double-edged practice:[53] the control of knowledge and truth (e.g., clinical medicine as a discipline), and the control of bodies and persons for social purposes (e.g., the use of medical and economic theory to discipline the size and behavior of population).

What was new, in the eighteenth century, was that by being combined and generalized, [the disciplines] attained a level at which the formation of knowledge and the increase of power regularly reinforce one another in a circular process. At this point the disciplines cross the 'technological' threshold. First the hospital, then the school, then, later, the workshop were not simply 'reordered' by the disciplines; they became, thanks to the disciplines, apparatuses such that any mechanism of objectification could be used in them as an instrument of subjection, and any growth of power could give rise in them to possible branches of knowledge; it was this link, proper to the technological systems, that made possible within the disciplinary element the formation of clinical medicine, psychiatry, child psychology, educational psychology, the rationalization of labor. It is a double process, then: an epistemological 'thaw' through a refinement of power relations; a multiplication of the effects of power through the formation and accumulation of new forms of knowledge.[54]

In short, the Bachelardian stratum of Foucault becomes a limit, requiring a return to Marx by way of Nietzsche. Knowledge leads to power by way of language.

LANGUAGE.   Language is that point at which Foucault most clearly explains the function of limits in his thought. At the same time it is where his thought becomes least intelligible. History, knowledge; then language. Marx, Bachelard; then Nietzsche and Bataille.

We who read Foucault from outside his intellectual field are likely to find his discussions of history and knowledge relatively accessible. We, too, have been schooled in Marx, and more recently, the *Annales* historians. If we are less familiar with Bachelard, this deficit is partly overcome by our familiarity with the history of science, an acquaintance due in large part to Thomas Kuhn, whatever his differences from Bachelard. But language is another matter. Social theorists outside France and Italy have scarcely penetrated as far as Saussure and Lévi-

Strauss. As a result, it is bewildering to encounter the unfamiliar names of Foucault's theory of language: Bataille, Blanchot, Roussel, Sade. Even Nietzsche remains a strange figure on North American horizons.

The problem, however, is not that of poorly informed readers. Language as such is near the limit of the intelligible in Foucault. Intelligibility, for Foucault, is a necessary limit. It is idealism's central project. Positivism, phenomenology, historicism—the methods against which Foucault rages[55]—all fail to grasp the concreteness of events because they overvalued intelligibility and undervalued error and the limit. Knowledge is not at the center, but on the margins of life; not within Man and his world, but at their limit; ultimately, at the point of death. Language and death—a perplexing association. It is, however, the relation within which Foucault develops his most complete theory of history, knowledge, discourse, and power.

Structuralist semiotics separated language from expression and meaning. It rejected the idea that language is, simply, a product of the speaking subject. Structuralism, it has been said many times, cuts language loose from consciousness. In so doing, it posed the question of the forms of language as such. Foucault shared these convictions without ever being infatuated by them. From the beginning he went beyond language as such. When asked to situate his theory of language historically and ideologically, Foucault said:

I am at the difference from those we call structuralists for I am not very interested in the formal possibilities offered by a system like language (*la langue*). Personally, I am above all haunted by the existence of discourses, by the fact that speaking has taken place as events in relation to their original situation, and that they have left behind traces which continue to exist and exercise, in their very subsistence internal to history, a certain numer of manifest or secret functions.[56]

When he asks, what is language?[57] he asks not of the meaning, essence, or form of language. Foucault's questions are of the existence, functioning, and practice of language. Hence, except for the historical studies in *The Order of Things*, his semiotic (if the term can be used at all) is almost exclusively applied to literature. Literature is both that which signaled the end of the Classical Age,[58] and that strange practice of language which, in the hands of Sade, Nietzsche, Bataille, Roussel, Artaud, Mallarmé, Blanchot brings language to the void.[59] "We are studying statements at the limit that separates them from what is not said . . ."[60] The positivity of literature, for Foucault, is not its form, but its ability to confront us with the relationship between language and human life. Literature, ironically, can lead to the silence which makes discourse possible. "What is this language that says nothing, is never silent, and is called 'literature'?"[61] Put crudely, literature is that language which, in spite of occasional pretenses to the contrary, can never represent reality. It is, thereby, language free to say any and everything. In attempting to do so it realizes that everything cannot be said. Language in literature must encounter the silence within which language exists. Literature, thus, must discover the futility of realism at the same moment it discovers the fact that Man, like God, is dead.

Cryptic? Confusing? Absurd? Yes, but it is not nonsense. Since Foucault wants to explain the limits of language, he cannot rely, purely and simply, on ordinary language to express himself. Thus, it is not reasonable to ask Foucault to be "clear" and mean by that: "Tell me in my words what you mean." Such a demand would be the same as asking Nietzsche what Zarathustra meant. Such a demand is in a language that Foucault, following Nietzsche, seeks to overcome.

It helps somewhat to notice that Foucault's discussions of language, limit, and death are nearly always marked by two series of names.[62] The one, more familiar, is Nietzsche, Marx, Freud. The other, less familiar, is Sade, Nietzsche, Mallarmé, Artaud, Bataille, Roussel, Blanchot, Klossowski, and Deleuze. Nietzsche's is a shifter between the two, without being an organizing center.[63] One may begin with Nietzsche, knowing however that Foucault will not rest with him.

Nowadays I prefer to remain silent about Nietzsche. . . . If I wanted to be pretentious, I would give "the genealogy of morals" as the general title of what I am doing. It was Nietzsche who specified the power relation as the general focus, shall we say, of philosophical discourse—whereas for Marx, it was the production relation. Nietzsche is the philosopher who has moreover been able to think power without having to confine himself within a political theory in order to do so . . . Nietzsche's contemporary presence is increasingly important. But I am tired of people studying him only in order to produce the kind of commentaries that are written on Mallarmé and Hegel. For myself, I prefer to utilize the writers I like. The only valid tribute to thought such as Nietzsche's is precisely to use it, to deform it, to make it groan and protest. And if then commentators say that I am being faithful or unfaithful to Nietzsche, that is of absolutely no interest.[64]

Foucault takes exactly the same attitude toward Nietzsche, as he does toward Marx. Close to Nietzsche, without being Nietzschean.

In relation to Marx and Freud, Nietzsche was an initiator of modern discourse.[65] Each performed an essential decentering functioning. All three attacked the notion of the Origin. All three employed a method which freed thought from an organizing, originating principle. All three put interpretation to work on an infinite series of relations: the relations of production and the theory of values in Marx, the relations of desire and the language of dreams in Freud, the relations of values and the Eternal Return in Nietzsche. All three methods rejected the absolute, controlling Sign. In all three values, rationality and consciousness are dethroned, and placed in a series of relations. All three opened the question of infinity. For this reason all three were immediately and rigorously resisted by the guardians of liberal ideology, those who defend the view that history "is living and continuous, that it is, for the subject in question, a place of rest, certainty, reconciliation, a place of tranquilized sleep."[66] Against the anthropological sleep, Marx, Freud, and Nietzsche saw Man as the product of relations which outrun him. Man was seen against death: alienation in

Marx, desire in Freud, wandering in Nietzsche. Life is "that which must forever surpass itself."[67]

In Nietzsche, the wanderer, Zarathustra, is he who speaks—against the will to truth, for the will to power. Power replaces truth and morality as the basic relation. For Nietzsche, this discovery was based on the transformation of language.

The guide-post which first put me on the *right* track was this question—what is the true etymological significance of the various symbols of the idea 'good' which have been coined in various languages. I then found that they all led back to *the same evolution of the same idea*—that everywhere "aristocrat," "noble," (in the social sense), is the root idea, out of which have necessarily developed "good" in the sense of "with aristocratic soul," "noble," in the sense of "with a soul of high calibre," "with a privileged soul"—a development which invariably runs parallel with that other evolution by which "vulgar," "plebian," "low" are made to change finally into "bad."[68]

In other words, Nietzsche's philology led to sociology. Nietzsche's genealogy was a study of the language used to define the good. His study of the discursive practices of morality put the words "good," "bad," "evil," "truth," "God" in sociological terms. "Let us speak of this *new demand*: We need a *critique* of values, the *value of these values* is for the first time called into question—and for this purpose a knowledge is necessary of the conditions and circumstances out of which these values grew . . ."[69] The idea "good" could no longer transcend man, and control his thought and being. "Good" is a social and political term, employed in the maintenance of a social order. The term "good," however, can be seen for what it is only when language is freed from its classical function: to express the truth of being. Thus, the liberation of language is coterminous with the death of God, where God, in modern terms, stands for all metaphysical principles of ultimate order. Thus, further, the death of God and the death of Man are coterminous. The infinite play of language, the deconstruction of morality, the critique of metaphysics, and the man who wanders on the precipice between the will to power and the void of death are the crux of Nietzsche's philosophy of power.[70] Hence, in simple terms, the association of language and death.

Foucault, however, situates Nietzsche in a second series. "Attraction is for Blanchot what is, without doubt, for Sade desire, for Nietzsche power, for Artaud the materiality of thought, for Bataille transgression: the pure experience of exteriority (de dehors) and the most naked of experiences."[71] In these relations, Nietzsche's will to power is placed, more explicitly, in the context of death and sexuality. "Perhaps the emergence of sexuality in our culture is an event of multiple values: it is tied to the death of God and to the ontological void which his death fixed at the limit of our thought."[72] In Sade, for example, three events dominate: the telling of tales, violent sexuality, and death without meaning.[73] Discourse, freed from the constraint of morality, leads inevitably to a violent transgression of morality, and man is left facing death—a void without meaning. Torture and murder in Sade do not express meaningful truths. They state, purely and simply, the limits of the human.

For Bataille, similarly, sexuality is at the heart of the human. Sexual creatures, in contrast to the asexual, reproduce by creating discontinuity out of continuity. The sperm and the ovum, discontinuous entities, become one at conception. "A continuity comes into existence between them to form a new entity from the death and disappearance of the separate beings."[74] The new creature who is born is, however, ultimately discontinuous from the parents. "On the most fundamental level there are transitions from continuous to discontinuous and from discontinuous to continuous. We are discontinuous beings, individuals who perish in isolation in the midst of an incomprehensible adventure, but we yearn for our lost continuity."[75] Thus, we see in Bataille what was in Nietzsche and is everywhere in Foucault. Analysis takes place between doublets. The fundamental fact of humanity is the irreconcilability of continuity and discontinuity,[76] to which Bataille relates the ironic dependence of eroticism on reproduction. Eroticism, by its very nature, is sexuality without regard to the instrumentality of reproduction. But, eroticism—emotional, physical, and religious—is predicated on the discontinuity created by the fact of our reproduction. Eroticism is a form of communication in which man searches for lost continuity. Ultimately eroticism is sacred, hence religious, communication. It is the search for eternal continuity. But, in effect, the search for God is based on the death of God, the fundamental fact of difference. In trying erotically to overcome discontinuity we discover only limits. As a result, eroticism is the most fundamental political act. Social limits are broken because of our natural condition. "Eroticism always entails a breaking down of established patterns, the patterns, I repeat, of the regulated social order basic to our discontinuous mode of existence . . ."[77]

Transgression, then, is not sexual license. It concerns knowledge and power, which are expressed in the conditions of sexuality. Prohibition is the means of social power for controlling knowledge and social action.[78] Transgression, therefore, recognizes that knowledge and the will to power are a duplicitous and necessary relation. Transgression is both at and against the limits of the social, where human knowledge and power are revealed. "Transgression suspends a taboo without suppressing it."[79] Man remains a social animal, while the facts of his animality compel him to seek his limit. He finds not God, but death. God's death and man's death entail each other as they make knowledge and power possible.

These deaths cut language loose from meaning. Man, without God or the transcendental Subject, can no longer express the inherent meaning of the world. These deaths make language an infinity of relations in which man, facing a void, lives at his limits. His knowledge, including self-knowledge, is necessarily exposed to power relations. Morality is replaced by politics.

This series of ideas, from Nietzsche and Sade through Bataille and Blanchot, explains much about Foucault's method and the sense of the strange one encounters in his writings. He is trying to do a history of knowledges with respect to a theory of language which theory is ultimately political. His earlier discussions of Bataille, and Nietzche, and Blanchot[80] are not so far as one might think from his much later studies of power and knowledge. The discussion of life, death, sexuality, and power-knowledge at the end of *The History of Sexuality* is explicitly political. But these politics are predicated on a conviction found in those much earlier, and seemingly apolitical literary and philosophical studies. Their political value is in the subtlety with which they examine the complexity of power. Foucault's politics are not those of a critical theorist attacking the visible world of power relations. The problem of power is internal to society. Power is within knowledge, as knowledge is within power. The economic fact will do no more than the idealist philosophy that science is free from error and ideology, or the historicist assumption of meaningful continuity apart from material fact. When knowledge and power are separated, we fall prey to the liberal illusion of liberation and freedom. We are unable to see, behind appearances, the fact that liberated man is, in fact, caught up in a power he himself sustains. Liberalism is the myth of Man, who, in his finitude, knows himself because he can imagine Himself. The transcendental Subject has many forms: the will to truth, positivist realism, phenomenological radicalization of identity theory, the elite theory of power, humanist morality. Each, in its way, controls no less than classical metaphysics, because each ignores or denies the truth of power. Power is not a Center, a Source, an Origin, a Truth, an Imposing Force. Power is relational. Power is that which we encounter when we accept the fact that man is difference, not unity. The authentically powerful man is one who recognizes his limit but refuses to overcome it transcendentally by projecting Man into the place formerly held by God. The will to power is the will to wander, to transgress those limits which cannot be overcome.

History, knowledge, and language are the apparent topical domains of Foucault's work. History is not calm continuity, but conflict and chance. Knowledge is not identity and truth, but

error and the experience of the no. Language is not representation and expression, but an infinity of signs which bring man
to his limit. They all meet, eventually, in power: the power to
know, to speak, and to transgress the very taboos man places
on himself. Taboo is society. Critical social theory is not
transcendence of the social, but transgression. Zarathustra was
a wanderer, not a thinker. Truth is in power. Theory is politics.

2. Method / HISTORICAL ARCHAEOLOGY

A RCHAEOLOGICAL METHOD. What could possibly be the relation between archaeology and historical method? Is this a metaphor suggesting various aspects of a method? Digging, uncovering layers, unearthing material objects, allowing archival fragments to stand for the whole, reconstructing lost civilizations. Or, at the other extreme, is this archaeology a model defining a formal method for the human sciences? Rules for specifying objects, correlating relations, setting boundaries, assessing documents. In other words, is archaeology figurative, or literal? Is Foucault toying with our imagination, suggesting, without recommending, a new way of looking at history? Or is he defining a program for recruits to a new social science? Is he, after all, in the lineage of Jarry, Artaud, Bataille, Nietzsche? Or, perhaps, that of Comte, Durkheim, Lévi-Strauss, Marx? Artist? Or scientist?

The answer is neither simply, yet both. Foucault's archaeology is figurative, but scientifically serious. It is literal, without being programmatic. His method is methodically different. Yet it is studiously serious. Its difference is precisely that it values a different space in which to pose historical and theoretical questions. The contents of this space are neither proofs, nor facts, nor interpretations. They are primarily, but not exclusively, discourse.

But this space is not the zero degree. Foucault's style is not white.[1] His style is often as elegantly complex as his contents are thickly descriptive. To be sure, Foucault's writing lacks the clarity of logic, the weight of fact, the depth of interpreted meaning. It has, in their stead, the density of the specific texts and documents he describes, and writes. To understand Foucault's method one best begins with his writing.

STYLE.   In Foucault's writing, the reader encounters three literary conventions which, among others, are the most persistent, striking, and unnerving. Being conventions, they are superficially natural to the reader. Each, however, is distorted, putting the reader again on the margin between the familiar and the strange. Described in terms of their surface effect, they are: the exceptional case, the oppositive structure, and the suppressed footnote.

First, every major text and most major sections within each text begin with the description of an exceptional case which acts as an anchor for what follows. *The Order of Things* commences with an elaborate description of Velázquez' painting *Las Meninas*, which introduces Foucault's analysis of the Renaissance episteme. Analogously, in the same book, Cervantes' Don Quixote presents the Classical Age. In *Discipline and Punish*, the gruesome details of Damiens' torture in 1757 describe Classical punishment, against which the birth of the disciplining prison of the nineteenth century is gradually described. *Birth of the Clinic* begins with passages from Pomme's, then Bayle's clinical records describing contrasting views of bodily membranes. The contrast sets the boundaries in time within which the teaching clinic was born. *The History of Sexuality* begins with the account of an anonymous, nearly ignored erotic memoir from the Victorian epoch, which serves to explode the assumption that, prior to Freud and modernity, sexuality was repressed. *Madness and Civilization* begins with the Ship of Fools in order to set the outer limits of the time when madness was confined to unreason. Even *Archaeology of Knowledge*, for all its relative abstractness, begins with an oddity, the statement (*l'énnoncé*) as the unit of discursive analysis.

These cases are exceptional in their concreteness. They do not serve to capture the spirit of their epoch. They are not totalizing devices. Their specificity is not, thereby, determined by the power, normality, importance, or fame of the event described. Velázquez and Damiens are not on the same level of cultural recognition. They are, simply, described instances which are used by Foucault to begin, then structure, his texts. Though occasionally annoyed by this device,[2] the persevering reader soon realizes that these are not cases at all. They do not stand for a larger category. Neither statistical members of an aggregated class, nor significant representatives of general propositions, nor poignant illustrations of a cultural totality, these strange beginnings do not point to something outside Foucault's text. Their effect is within the text. They bring into what is written the concrete details of the larger structures Foucault presents. In their specificity, they are sufficient unto themselves. The Velázquez painting in *The Order of Things*, for example, neither represents nor illustrates the Renaissance episteme. It is that episteme in its significant detail because, as we shall see, it is a true product of a discursive formation in which no one instance is privileged over another.

Second, Foucault regularly employs the oppositive structure. "Then . . . , now . . . ," "Not . . . , but . . . ," "in the Renaissance . . . , but in the Classical Age . . ." are crucial organizing structures, especially at the end of chapters and sections where Foucault carefully summarizes in order to return the reader to the general theme. The beginnings invoked by exceptional cases are eventually organized within a careful comparative method. As a result, nothing stands alone. Everything is relational. The exceptional case is extraordinary only when one reads with the formal standards of statistical significance or hermeneutical representativeness in mind. Within the text, the exceptional is put into a comparative relationship with other specific cases. Hence comparison does not serve to illuminate and expose the continuous threat of a progressive history. Comparison binds and limits the structures of a history in which no one epoch is decisively privileged over another.

Third, Foucault avoids excessive documentation, almost to the point of compulsion. This too annoys the impatient reader who, with greater care, would find that documentation exists. Though sparse, there are footnotes. Though sparingly used, there are dates. Though secondary to the exceptional cases, there are chronicles. Documentation is used parsimoniously, as if to displace attention from the science in his work, opening a place for its art. But documentation is there as if to protect a place for his science. *Birth of the Clinic*, for example, is a tightly argued history of fewer than a hundred years in medical science. The reader must carefully check the dates of Syndenham, Pinel, Bayle, Broussait, and Bichat in order to discover the distinctions. Even though the dates are crucial they are seldom provided in the text. The reader must check them, usually in the bibliography, often by consulting an encyclopedia. The reader is forced to do his own work. Unlike scientific texts, the author refuses his responsibility to expose the truth of things; but, equally, unlike artistic texts, the reader is not allowed into the raw, inspiring truth of pure art. One senses that this trick has something to do with Foucault's self-characterization: "I am not an artist, I am not a scientist. I am somebody who tries to deal with reality through those things which are always, often, far from reality."[3]

"Always, often, far from reality . . ." This is as basic to Foucault's literary form as to his historical method. The literary devices are not what they seem to be. Not the use of exceptional cases; not simply a comparative or dialectic method; not an obstinate refusal to document. But stylistic conventions dictated by a method situated between art and science.

METHOD.   What then is this space far from reality? Simply put, it is the space of relations between rules and practices.

It is not a space in which rules govern practices. The rules in question are not laws, values, norms. They are not positive or analytic abstractions. They are not the action of state or civil society on the individual, any more than they are an inherent grammar of social action. They are plural. Rules and practices. In their plurality, they are specific. The rules and regularities: Foucault plays with the semantic tension between the rule (*la regle*) and the regular (*la regularité*). In so doing, he refuses the extremes of the transcendent, abstract rule which governs and the statistical norm which averages. He is asking a concrete question. What are the forces and relations which allow us, from time to time, to observe regularities in the variance of the historical world? The world is not pure variance. Foucault wants to account for the order in this variance without relying on the essence of rules, or an empiricism of statistical averages. Between the extremes of overly structural and overly positivistic histories, Foucault wants to explain concrete practices. Formalist history makes practices ciphers in a system of ideas. Interpretivist history takes practices as transparent signs through which is read a teleology of meaning. Positivist history accumulates practices as context-free facts. In each case what is said or what is done is reduced away. The struggle of historical action is tamed. By contrast, Foucault insists that "the historicity which conveys and determines us is bellicose. . . ."[4] Formalist history pacifies history under the blanket of organizing ideas. Interpretivist history sublimates its bellicosity by projecting it on the pretentiously deeper struggle of secret meanings. Positivist history prudishly ignores it. Against these tactics, Foucault wants to maintain the concrete struggle of history. "History does not have any 'meaning' which does not mean it is absurd, incoherent. On the contrary, it is intelligible and must have the capacity to be analyzed down to the smallest detail; but according to the intelligibility of struggles, strategies, and tactics."[5]

What specifically are these practices? They are the concrete events around which Foucault's books are written. In *Madness and Civilization*, not madness as such, but the practice of confining the mad in the Classical Age. In *Birth of the Clinic*, not medicine as such, but the practice of clinical knowledge and morbid anatomy in the nineteenth century. In *The Order of Things*, not science as such, but the discursive practices which gave rise to the human sciences in the nineteenth century. In *Discipline and Punish*, not punishment as such, but the practices of discipline and correction in which the modern prison was born. In *History of Sexuality*, not sexuality as such, but the medical, pedagogical, psychiatric, and economic practices which regulated the sexuality of women, children, the family, and the perverse in the modern era.

Just as they are not abstractions, practices are not, in their concreteness, arbitrary, accidental effluents of free motives. Practices are regulated. Not by the enforcing power of rules, nor by the inner control of knowledge. Practices are regulated by power and knowledge; both, at once. Power and knowledge rule and regulate. They cannot be divorced from each other. "Two words sum up everything: power and knowledge."[6] Confining the mad involved the knowledge that madness belongs to unreason; confinement was necessary for the politics of a bourgeois social order. The practice of clinical medicine depended upon the knowledge produced by the clinical gaze; and was made possible by an economic liberalism which, simultaneously, freed the physician to examine the patient's body, while subtly confining the ill bodies of the poor to the teaching clinic. Discipline, in the nineteenth century, involved knowledge of the correctability of the soul in paradoxical relation to the social need to create an economically productive delinquent class. Sexuality was in part deployed in the form of a Malthusian knowledge of the social pathology of excessive births, but also for the political purpose of producing a controlled balance between a disciplined labor force and a limited population of consumers.

Though Foucault has gradually refined his theory of the relationship between knowledge and power, all his works assume that history studies practices which are the products of their interplay. By the time of *History of Sexuality* the concepts merge. They become power-knowledge (*pouvoir-savoir*). Foucault is well aware of the dangers on both sides of this formulation. Just as idealist history of ideas holds that power relations are the products of great ideas or cultural totalities, so the Marxist materialism prominent in Foucault's Paris believes that knowledge is in the last instance determined by economic power relations. For Foucault, practices are neither articulations of knowledge, nor epiphanies of power relations. Foucault sets himself between Hegel and Althusserian Marxism.[7]

What then is this space far from reality? Obviously not appearances. Practices, such as confinement, clinical medicine, or birth control, are not what they appear to be. For years the themes of punishment and correction were confused in the practice of confinement. Likewise, clinical medicine was suspended between the classificatory medicine which preceded it and the medicine of pathological reactions which, eventually, completed its revolution. And the control of births appeared to be the repressive manipulation of the family, when it was even more the positive deployment of sexuality.

Practices are not on the surface intelligible. Such a naive view leads down the same blind alley in which modern social psychology has been trapped. If motives cause behaviors, why do not measures of attitudes predict behaviors? If behaviors can be counted as equivalent to attitudes, then why are there counterintuitive effects? For Foucault the intelligibility of practices has nothing to do with the intentions of actors, or with the surface regularity of the practice itself. The intelligibility of history is entirely at the margin of appearances. Without denying appearances, the apparent must be overcome in order to define its limits. In *Birth of the Clinic*, for example, the specificity of the practice of clinical medicine (new ways of looking at tissues, a new seriousness in perceiving the body, the elaboration of morbid anatomy, a new relationship between life and death, a new theory of fevers, and so forth) is made intelligible by discovering the limits of clinical medicine.

To take the examination of bodies at face value would not isolate the modern clinic. Indeed, from the point of view of continuous history the clinic would appear only as a step in the progress of the history of medicine, a history with Hippocrates as its Origin. But Foucault insists that during the Classical Age the patient's body was little more than a semantic support for the classification of diseases. Moreover, he shows that when the modern clinic was born it was necessary to rewrite the history of medicine in order to reinsert the patient in the history of the physician at the bedside. For most if not all of this history, the patient was incidental to the necessity of competing systems of medical theory.[8]

The space far from reality within which Foucault works is that between practices and regularities in which the regularities that make practices intelligible can never themselves be purely visible. Neither rules nor norms, regularities are the longer terms of historical struggle that define the limits of practices. The body upon which the practicing physician's gaze came to rest early in the nineteenth century was made possible by a series of conflicts. One series passed through medicine: the conflict within the medical profession between the Royal Society of Medicine and the university medical faculty. One passed through knowledge (*savoir*) and the disciplines (*connaissances*): the conflict between rational classifying knowledge and the liberated observing knowledge of the nineteenth century. One passed through politics: the doctor as an agent of the new state's quest for a perfectly healthy populace able to fulfill the liberal ideal of a democratized, working social body. One passed through the economy: the segregation of a working class, which in health provided labor power, and in sickness provided for the clinic the bodies subjected to the medical gaze. Each of these series of conflicts must be described. They are the historical layers isolated by Foucault's archaeology. They are not uniform. They have different times. No single one is privileged over the others. The economic series is not necessarily more determining, in a specific case, than the political or the epistemological. But when each is described the space of a regularity is defined. The result is neither a rule, nor a proposition, nor a total picture of a society. It is a series of series, fully described, which fills the space behind the visible practice of clinical observations.

What is this space behind and in tension with visible practices? It is not, most definitely, a place of secrets to be interpreted by the historian. Neither analogies leading to a totalizing spirit of the times; nor a psychoanalysis seeking the inner, psychological truth of the visible.[9] In fact, the error of interpretivism helps define the limits of Foucault's method. To interpret is to comment on the visible. To comment is to write a supplementary text which presents the deeper meaning hidden in the original document or event. Interpretation correctly assumes that the primary event cannot be taken at face value; but, incorrectly, it assumes that the inadequacy of the visible warrants the historian to reconstruct a deeper meaning. The error is that the primary object loses its specificity. It becomes a mere signifier of meanings. Historians must work with documents without destroying them. This is the attitude of the responsible archivist who each day delicately turns those fragile, aged pages. If torn or soiled they are lost forever. If excessively interpreted they are, no less, lost to history. The historian respects his documents, all the while realizing they do not tell the whole truth. Since the whole truth is not told, positivistically, by the document, the problem is: How can the historian preserve the document, yet make it intelligible? He must refer to that which is not in the document in order to explain the document without destroying its positivity. For history the document is there. It is all that is there. Yet it is insufficient. Its intelligibility is at the margin transgressed originally by the writing of the document, then transgressed by the historian's reconstructions.

We have, it is true, subtly but necessarily introduced another term, the *document*. We have slipped into an equation. Documents were substituted for practices. Discursive practices for practices is not however an equation of identity. Foucault does not believe that the world is purely and simply discourse. Rather, he faces the specific problem of a working historian. For history, and equally for all the human sciences, one works only with discursive practices, documents. Hence the practice of clinical medicine, or of correction and punishment, or of general grammar in the classical age, is visible only by means of the documents written by Bayle, Broussait, Tuke, Condillac. The visible history is the document (Bayle's clinical records), itself an instance of the practices (clinical medicine) studied. The document must not be referred to Bayle's intentions or the ethos of the late eighteenth and early nineteenth centuries, but to the practice itself. This reconstruction, however, must be done positively, which, for Foucault, is possible only with reference to one basic question. Why was this and not something else said? "We are studying documents at the limit that separates them from what is not said. . . ."[10]

The centrality of discourse in Foucault's method is less a philosophical principle than a practical requirement of historical research. One of Foucault's contributions is to have opened up discourse as such as the unavoidable resource and topic of historical research.[11] No historian can avoid the primacy of the document. Foucault has given this fact a positive place in historical methodology. He has done so by means of a simple, yet compelling, conclusion. The document is a practice of discourse produced by the same conflicts and struggles which produced social practices like those of clinical medicine. For the historian there is no meaningful distinction between the two. Bayle's clinical records are not synechdochically a mere part of the whole of clinical medicine. Documents are not rhetorical. They are practices on the same level as other medical practices of the time. They can be read only at their limit, only by reconstructing the regulating forces which produced them.

This, then, is the space within which Foucault works. The space between practices and rules is the space in which social relations determine what can and cannot be said in discourse.

It is the space in which one must ask: Why was this and not something else said? Hence, the description of regularities is a description of mechanisms for the deployment and exclusion of discursive practices. Though in his early work Foucault emphasized exclusion, he balanced the agenda in *Discipline and Punish* and *History of Sexuality*. Regulation is both an imposition of forces prohibiting certain practices and a grid (*dispositif*) of forces included in practices. In simple terms, society does not just rule out certain practices. It works because actors accept and maintain, in their actions, what is known to be acceptable action. Or, in different terms, power excludes what is not said; and it selects what is said. Similarly, knowledge is that which is excluded; and it is that which is found in what is said. Power-knowledge is not an abstraction. It is practices. As practices, it is only intelligible by means of the concrete historical conditions that rule and regulate, exclude and include what is done, what is said. These are power-knowledge.

Practices/rules, visible/invisible, power/knowledge. These conceptual couples are necessary to each other. Practices are visible, rules (and regularities) are not. Rules are not the action of society on actors, but the conditions within which action takes place. Power, thereby, is not rule imposition, but practices. Knowledge is not a passive attribute of social competence, it is practices. Power, because it cannot be separated from knowledge, is both that which dominates and that which selects. Power-knowledge is neither visible nor invisible. Because it is practiced it is visible, because it regulates it is not clearly visible. The regulating effect of power-knowledge must be described in order to explain practices. It can only be described, by the historian, by means of documents which neither fully reveal nor conclusively hide the regulating mechanisms. Likewise, regulation is never simply the action of the political economy on ideas; nor of ideas expressed in a political economy. History is conflict and struggle. Action is tactical and strategic. A bellicose history cannot be read by means of abstractions or systems of thought; nor by meaningful interpretations. History must be read in documents produced by these conflicts. Documents are visible, readable, practices regulated by specific relations at a specific time, which relations are the regulating and regularizing forces of society.

We see, therefore, that discourse is central to Foucault's method not because he is a semiotician, but because he is an historian. He makes this clear in the *History of Sexuality*:

What is to be said about sex must not be analyzed simply as the surface projection of these power mechanisms. Indeed, it is in discourse that power and knowledge are joined together. And for this very reason, we must conceive discourse as a series of discontinuous segments whose tactical function is neither uniform nor stable. To be more precise, we must not imagine a world of discourse divided between accepted discourse and excluded discourse or between dominant discourse and the dominated one; but as a multiplicity of discursive elements . . . in various strategies. It is this distribution that we must reconstruct, with the things said and those concealed, the enunciations [*énnociations*] required and those forbidden, that it comprises . . ."[12]

If it is in discourse that power and knowledge are joined together, this is because historical struggle takes place in discourse. Ironically, this view is a consequence of Foucault's desire to broaden the historian's perspective. He attacks the notion that history is the history of great events: battles, elections, regencies, discoveries, royal decisions. Events such as these, the stuff of traditional history, are events only superficially. The conflicts leading to Louis XVI's decline, to Napoleon's defeat at Waterloo, to Robespierre's execution are too often taken as events without contexts. Ideologies and power plays are abstracted from the ongoing hidden conflicts which, in daily life, sustained, then defeated, Louis XVI, Napoleon, and Robespierre. These were conflicts in discourse: in courtly rumor, in secrets passed in cafés, in alliances amongst merchants, in soldiers' complaints. Discourse cannot be stratified. Robespierre's speeches did not count for more than the talk of the masses which helped to bring him down. Power-knowledge, fully understood, is not exhaustively expressed in the great events. The real and fundamental conflicts of history are those that extend throughout the levels of a social formation. They are the conflicts created and conveyed in daily talk, in communiqués and messages, in orders, in orders defied, in rumor, and the like. "Discursive practices are not purely and simply ways of producing discourse. They are embodied in technical processes, in institutions, in patterns of general behavior, in forms for transmission and diffusion, in pedagogical forms which at once, impose and maintain them."[13] Yes, society is more than discourse. But it is in and by means of discourse that social conflict takes place.

Hence, the influence of the *Annales* tradition. History must account for events. But events can only be explained with reference to long enduring material, economic, and social histories. Foucault uses discourse to provide access to the long terms of social and economic history. Foucault, however, tries to escape a dilemma of the *Annales* method. How does one prevent structures from becoming an abstract destiny that determines events? Or, stated with respect to discourse, how can one analyze discursive practices without lapsing into a formal analysis of language (*la langue*) or an empiricist observation of what is said (*la parole*)? The answer is found in that most perplexing of Foucault's ideas, discontinuity.

Foucault is an opponent of linear, evolutionist history. But he does not mean by discontinuous history periodizations marked by dramatic ruptures in which all that went before is absent in what follows. Foucault's alternative is best summarized in his Nietzschean idea of the event.

Effective (*wickliche*) history deals with events in terms of their most unique characteristics, their most acute manifestations. An event, consequently, is not a decision, a treaty, a reign, or a battle, but the reversal of a relationship of forces, the usurpation of power, the appropriation of a vocabulary turned against those who had once used it, a feeble domination that poisons itself as it grows lax, the entry of a master "other." The forces operating in history are not controlled by destiny or regulative mechanisms, but respond to haphazard conflicts. They do not manifest the successive forms of a primordial intention and their attraction is not that of a conclusion, for they always appear through the singular randomness of events.[14]

Discontinuity has less to do with absolute political or epistemological ruptures than with concrete events dispersed in time and space. Events are "a reversal of a relationship of forces." As such they are not necessarily more evident in treaties, battles, and decisions than in immanent "'local centers' of power-knowledge." In the history of sexuality one example is the discourse by which children were sexualized: "The body of the child, under surveillance, surrounded in his cradle, his bed, or his room by an entire watch-crew of parents, nurses, servants, educators and doctors, all attention to the least manifestation of his sex, has constituted, particularly since the eighteenth century, another 'local center' of power-knowledge."[15]

Foucault seems to be saying that the battle or treaty event is made possible by concrete events that occur in mundane settings, at a child's cradle, a patient's bedside, a prison cell. The historian uncovers reversals in force relations by discovering, in documents, moments when what previously was not said is said and what was said is no longer said. In other words, events are, in large part, reversals in discursive practices. They occur by means of a shift at the margin between apparent reality and that space beyond reality, between the visible and the hidden, the familiar and the strange. Hence, discontinuity is not simply an interruption of the line of historical progress. It is what the *Annales* historians call a conjuncture. It is a reversal brought about by the rearrangement of the various layers of power-knowledge. All dimensions of society do not change at once, uniformly. In the history of the clinic, medical knowledge changed more slowly than the politics of medicine. The new physician was made necessary by requirements of the state and the medical profession some years before the knowledge of fevers was able to give clinical medicine a coherent theory of disease. But, in the history of punishment, the idea of moral correction preceded the discovery of the economic value of the prison's delinquent class. Likewise, in the history of sexuality, positive knowledge of sexuality began in the thirteenth-century Christian confessional. The political-economic interest in sexuality's relationship to a working population did not arise until the nineteenth century.

History, for Foucault, moves on a number of different levels: the epistemological, the medical, the political, the pedagogical, the psychological, the economic, and so forth. Each archaeological level has its own time. Changes in one do not necessarily cause changes in the others. The event is the moment of a coming together of rearrangements of the relations of these levels. The relations comprising power-knowledge in a society change when there is a new definition of the conflict and struggle of history. In one case the event is present initially in an epistemological practice; in another, in a new clinical practice; in another, in a new political practice. Once power-knowledge has changed, changes in the various archaeological levels occur in their own, overlapping times. The historian's event is the sufficient moment when the reversal is uncovered. Events are read in reversals of discursive practices. Though, obviously, they have effects, in time, throughout the range of social practices.

Foucault's histories, therefore, are histories of events understood by means of restructurings of the archaeological layers of society which, in their relationships to each other, regulate practices. Foucault's histories, hence, are histories explaining the birth of new practices: the confinement of the mad, psychiatry, the observation of the patient's body, morbid anatomy, the human sciences, the modern prison, the deployment of panoptical architecture, the treatment of sexual perversions, the control of births.

It is possible now to see that the stylistic features of Foucault's writing are consistent with his method. His literary use of the exceptional case, the oppositive structure, the suppressed footnote are corollaries to a history of exceptional dispersed events. This is a history that must isolate the exceptional because in the exceptional one finds the reversal of forces regulating practices. Since the reversal is a complex restructuring, it must be described comparatively. The "then" and "now" surrounding the event must be described in order to set the limits of the event. Since the event is a product of struggle among structures and forces reconstructed by means of documents, footnotes are not of the essence. Descriptions are. The reader is pulled back into the space, far from reality, wherein the struggle of history constantly transforms regulatory forces. Footnotes cannot define the margin between what is said and not said. The reader must see, in Foucault's descriptions, the invisible visibility of regulated practices.

FACT AND KNOWLEDGE.   There is, however, a fourth troubling stylistic attribute, Foucault's vocabulary. Why episteme instead of paradigm? Why force relations instead of class relations? Why archaeology instead of history? Why event instead of conjuncture? Why practice instead of act? Why the regular instead of structure or order? And why those other lexical inventions which have no apparent analogues: statement, archive, historical a priori, dispersion, enunciative modality, and so forth?

Foucault cannot be read, without revision, in the language of his sources. His vocabulary is neither Marxian, nor Nietzschean; neither psychoanalytic, nor Bachelardian; neither that of the *Annales* tradition; nor of Blanchot. Yet, as always, somehow something of each. Lecourt has asked, for example, why was it necessary for Foucault to create this strange vocabulary when his trajectory is so parallel to that of Marxism?[16] Similarly, it is germane to ask, why did he not stay with the bounds of *Annales'* historiography, of Bachelard's history of science, of Nietzche's genealogy? Or, if compelled along another course, why does he pervert these themes by constantly disrupting their similarity with the originals?

We already know part of the answer. Foucault is doing

history in a space different from that of traditional social theory and history. His method requires him to refuse givens and rewrite history with reference to events. It is not that everything that has gone before is useless, but that it must be recast in order to preserve the specificity of events. It is as though the specificity of events can be preserved only by maintaining the specificity of his writing. He changes his own vocabulary from study to study. Though, surely, there is a hint of flare in his strange style, there is no less a clear methodological plan.

Foucault is doing the constructive work of identifying a new set of objects and boundaries for social history. He tries to work between the extremes of empiricism, wherein the visible exhausts signification, and idealism, wherein the hidden idea explains away the visible fact. In Bachelardian fashion, Foucault views these extremes as mirror images each of the other. For Foucault, their critique forms one axis of a methodological field. Critique is a constructive practice. One does not criticize empiricism and idealism in order to dismiss them, but to define, in the space of their errors, a necessary methodological rule. History must acknowledge the visible document as its first surface of investigation, but it cannot explain the document without recourse to that which is hidden thereupon. The historian must read the events chronicled on documents with reference to the field of long-enduring structures that produced them. Court records are produced by the complex power relations of the royal court. The historian has the records, but reads them with reference to these relations. But, at this moment, the idealist temptation is present. It is possible to see those records as a mere expression of those relations, of the ethos of a royal epoch. Hence idealism's error of undercutting the visible document, of reading records only for signified clues of an ideal model of courtly life and action. Such a totalizing image destroys the surface validity of the documents, which, taken collectively, are the only positive basis for describing court relations. Without the record of events, there is no description of structures. Without the structures there is no parsimonious or coherent way to read the records. History must work constantly between the extremes of the visible document and the hidden social field. That which is hidden is not absolutely invisible except in an idealist history of inner or transcendent truths, which, in fact, is not history at all. All history has, for every explanatory judgment, only documents at its disposal. It must guard against easily received great systems of truth, such as: Calvin gave rise to capitalism, Freud liberated us from repressed sexuality, clinical medicine began with Hippocrates, man has always existed as an object of thought. Received ideas must be used primarily as objects to be broken down and reconstructed in a continual return to documents. Without these ideas there would be pure document. With them, taken too seriously, there would be no document. This, in general terms, is the visible/hidden axis of Foucault's historical field.

Just as the hidden principles of ideal history and the visible documents of empirical history form an axis of tension, so is this axis in tension with another, similarly bipolar, dimension. If the first is the path along and within which fact is produced, the second is the line of knowledge. Knowledge as such is not at issue here. It would be wrong to think of this dimension as epistemology. Here Foucault is more concerned with conditions necessary for the production of knowledge. The errors Foucault here critiques are those which in formal language would be called absolutism and relativism. More accurately, they are order and free play. The pole of ordering, what Derrida would call the Center, is the error whereby knowledge overcontrols its content.[17] Systematizing, ontologizing, and formalizing are among its best known strategies. Here knowledge is understood as the action of controlling the variance of reality by means of an organizing table, scheme, principle, or system. It assumes that the clarity of the scheme whereby knowledge is represented should be privileged over the imperative of representing the complexity of that which is known. At the other extreme is knowledge that privileges the free play of ideas or facts. Relativism, at the extreme, would be the intellectual utopia in which knowledge represents all that can be said, all the relations and nuances bearing on that which is known. Precisely because the latter is utopia, while the former is the dominating metaphysics of Western thought, Foucault engages the principle of Order more frequently. In the process, he appears to be a relativist.[18] But, beneath appearances, it is clear that Foucault seeks a middle ground. He does so by means of discourse. Knowledge is material because it cannot be separated from discourse. The book and the oeuvre are dismissed.[19] But they must be employed because knowledge is produced in discourse. Hence, the textuality of knowledge provides the conditions within which what is said as knowledge must be ordered because it is confined by the page and the binding. Though this is the most elemental basis of order, it is inescapable. Books begin and end, if only awkwardly.[20] Systems and intellectual structures, first principles and axioms are, therefore, the temptation to superimpose, on the confined space of the text, a second artificial ordering of knowledge's words. There can be no absolute free play of discourse. All that might be said, cannot be said. Neither by the voice, nor the pen. Coherent knowledge must, of necessity, surpass the proposition, the sentence, or the speech act. Syntagmata must be cut, and shaped. The desire of free association, in which the unattainable ideal of free play is rooted, is shaped, at some minimal threshold. This is the condition of knowledge. Foucault seeks to decenter Western metaphysics by means of a theory of knowledge as discourse. He works between the unruly desire to speak without limit and the compulsion to control this free discourse by contextless principles of Order.

Foucault, therefore, works in a space formed by the intersection of multiple tensions among the hidden and the visible, order and free play. This is the point wherein historical discourse materializes knowledge by constructing, from documents, the hidden structures which give rise to fact.

ARCHAEOLOGY OF KNOWLEDGE.   Where does *Archaeology of Knowledge* fit in? Where in this methodological book are we to find these two axes? Granted one finds there the visible/invisible couple, the question of epistemic knowledge (*savoir*) and accumulated knowledge (*connaissances*), the concept discursive practice, the critique of systems, and the Center (or, the principles of the Author, the Origin, and so forth). But, by what right, do we introduce the axis of fact, and the dimension of knowledge production? Are they not interpreters' inventions?

It is easy, all too easy, to receive *Archaeology of Knowledge* as Foucault's methodological program. Except for several things. It comes neither at the beginning nor at the end of his work. Neither propädeutic, nor résumé, this book is more a gathering up of what has gone before, and a suggestion of what was to come thereafter. "Hence the cautious, stumbling manner of this text: at every turn, it stands back, measures up what is before it, gropes toward its limits, stumbles against what it does not mean, and digs pits to mark out its own path."[21] Nor is it presented as a programmatic statement. Yes, the rules of an archaeological history are defined. But, they are presented in such an unmethodic manner. There are the repetitions, the constant attack on the history of ideas, the oscillations between a disavowal of structuralism and a critique of hermeneutics' subjectivism.

There is, moreover, the duplicitous development of the book. First, discursive practices and regularities are stipulated, then the statement and the archive are introduced, finally archaeological description is discussed. On the surface this appears to be a natural evolution, from the unit, to the tool, to the technique. But, on closer reading, one realizes that this purely methodological development is caught up in another theme. The book is also topical. Its subject is knowledge (*savoir*), and knowledge's relationship to discourse. This becomes unmistakably clear in the concluding chapter of Part IV, "Science and Knowledge," which ends: "To the questions posed above— Is archaeology concerned only with sciences? Is it always an analysis of scientific discourse?—we can now give a reply, in each case in the negative. What archaeology tries to describe is not the specific structure of science, but the very different domain of *knowledge (savoir)*."[22] With this conclusion one is brought back to the very title of the book, *L'Archaeologie du savoir*. Beneath the description of method, this book is what its title says it is, a book on knowledge. Neither simply a program, nor an epistemology. But, quite plausibly, an archaeological description of the historian's knowledge, the problem which lies beneath the major books which came before, *Madness and Civilization, Birth of the Clinic*, and *The Order of Things*. We are, at this moment, reminded that all three of these books are preoccupied with the rise of modern knowledge and the decline of the classical age: Reason and unreason in the history of madness, medical perception and clinical knowledge, the human sciences. *Archaeology of Knowledge* is what it says it is. "My aim is to uncover the principles and consequences of an autochthonous transformation that is taking place in the field of historical knowledge."[23] But where does a text such as this fit in? "My aim . . ." says Foucault. What is the reference? "My aim . . ." Where? *Archaeology of Knowledge*? Or his work as a whole? It must be the latter. This declaration, we know, is from the Introduction to *Archaeology* and is a derivation of an earlier reflection on his work. It is part of an ongoing, intermittent response to questions;[24] an attempt to clarify for others, less than for himself, what he is attempting to do. Hence the anomalous relation of both the Introduction and the Conclusion to the remainder of this book. Neither the beginning nor the ending texts dwell on the special vocabulary of enunciative modalities, historical a priori, archive, the statement, and so forth. In fact, no other major text of Foucault employs these terms systematically. They are trapped, suspended, in this one book. It is as though the Introduction and the Conclusion serve to enclose and set off an archaeology of knowledge from the rest of Foucault's writings. Their style and content suggest this. Stylistically, they are more explicitly dialogic. The Introduction is a straightforward description of Foucault's sources, a reflection on his errors, and a passing response to false impressions of his position. All are responses to readings of his work. The Conclusion covers similar territory, though it is in the form of the Socratic dialogue. Foucault answers the charges of a nameless Other. In both he repeats his familiar rejection of the subjectivism of historicist hermeneutics, while adding, almost plaintively, a disavowal of structuralist objectivism. In these boundary texts, he is speaking to the world of his readers. "Do not ask who I am and do not ask me to remain the same: leave it to our bureaucrats and our police to see that our papers are in order."[25]

Between the Introduction and the Conclusion *Archaeology of Knowledge* has more to do with *savoir* than with Foucault. How else are we to explain the fact that its intricate vocabulary lacks both its density and frequency of appearance before and after this book?

Where does *Archaeology of Knowledge* fit in? Simply as a book that is exceptional in the same way as all Foucault's books are exceptional. *Archaeology* must not be measured against Foucault's literary trajectory, either as that which explains everything else, or as the rule-breaking exception. It is unusual, and for many partially unnaturalizable for reason of his style and his method. Foucault writes, in all his books, in an off-center discursive space. Decentered, yet not purely relativistic. Beneath the surface of the visible, yet not from the ideal heights (or depths) of undocumented structures (or meanings). Neither subjectivistic nor objectivistic. "We must avoid placing responsibility either simply in the individual or the economic."[26] Foucault writes of discursive practices with respect to a specific theory of discursive practice. Hence, the connection between his style and his method. He employs the exceptional case, the oppositive structure, while rejecting positivistic documentation. *Archaeology of Knowledge*, like his other works, is written in the exceptional space of Foucault's own discourse on the regularities governing the discourse in which knowledge is produced. This is neither pure surface, nor pure mystery; neither a given system of concepts, nor a maelstrom of relations. In effect it is the space of all socially responsible discourse. Discourse that refuses equally either to take appearances at face value or to found critique in a transcendental ideal. Discourse which seeks an appropriate and modest order between absolutistic and relativistic knowledge. As such it is always a discourse which must purchase validity on the tenuously sensible grounds of what can, must be, and is said. This space of practiced discourse is, of necessity, stated between opposites for the same reason that it refuses to gain comfort in an excess of visible documentations. Discourse behind the visible document and between the Center and the relative must be the concrete talk of positions taken between opposing discursive forces.

We can, of course, use *Archaeology of Knowledge*, but not to summarize or fix his method. It is neither representative, nor illustrative, but a specific practice regulated by the field of his work. The vocabulary of *Archaeology of Knowledge* is to Foucault's method, as *Las Meninas* and Damiens' execution are to *The Order of Things* and *Discipline and Punish*.

That bizarre, ill-defined concept—*the statement, l'énoncé*—bears all the marks of Foucault's method. It is the unit of discursive analysis, but it is not codifiable. It is a term borrowed, apparently, from linguistics. But it is much more than a set of articulated linguistic objects produced by the process of enunciation. For English readers it is caught in semantic suspension between the woeful inadequacy of "the enunciated," which is not said in this context, and the translator's invention, *the statement*, which unfortunately confuses the term's association with linguistics. *L'énoncé* is a term from linguistics, yet more. Statement is a term from common parlance, yet less. In English we can live with the empty term *statement*. The term will have its meaning only in the field of writing about and around it. Hence, we are not surprised to read that "the statement is neither visible nor hidden."[27] Nor, that its threshold "is the threshold of the existence of signs."[28] Nor, that its specificity is defined by Foucault comparatively: not a proposition, not a sentence, not a speech act.[29] And, finally, we are not surprised that it exists in a regulated field: "It must be related to a whole adjacent field."[30]

As a condition for the practice of discourse, the statement is on the dimension describing the production of knowledge. Similarly, on the axis of fact, it is situated at the very margin between visible discursive practices and the hidden regularities that condition practices. It allows observed practices their positivity, without reducing the positive to the visible. Without the statement historical facts would be stark observations of events, or measured values encoding those observations. Without the statement, it would be possible to see knowledge as an abstract ordering system, or an entropic relativity of events. Neither visible nor hidden. The statement is not Velázquez's *Las Meninas* or a sentence in Bayle's clinical record or Bentham's diagram of the panopticon. The statement is that which allowed Velázquez to paint, Bayle to write, and Bentham to draw as they did. The painting, the text, and the diagram are specific, and visible. Foucault wishes to avoid methodologies which could distract attention from specific events. He does not want the author to assume more concreteness than his practices. He does not want a system of ideas to tempt the reader away from the described events. He does not want methodology to be the object of controversy. Hence, he invents this translucent term. The statement, *l'énoncé*, lets light through but is not interesting in itself. Its translucence serves to protect the specificity of the practices described.

The lack of specificity of the concept statement protects the practices against formalist, positivist, or interpretivist ideas of rules. Practices are explained by their relationships to regularizing rules, for which Foucault reserves the term *archive*. An archive is not, literally, the totality of documents collected by a culture. Nor, metaphorically, is it the institutions within which documents are produced. "The archive is first the law of what can be said, the system that governs the appearance of statements as unique events."[31] Statement and archive play on either edge of the distinction between practice and regulation. The archive is an historical a priori: "Not a condition of validity for judgments, but a condition for the reality of statements."[32] If the statement is the condition for discursive practices, then the archive is the regulation within those conditions. "It is the general system of the formation and transformation of statements."[33] Practice/rule, visible/hidden, statement/archive. The archive is on the side of the hidden rule. "It is that which, outside ourselves, delimits us."[34] With the archive translucence becomes opaqueness. We can never, therefore, describe the archive of our present. It must be seen at a distance, from a point outside its own rules.

Hence, with the archive we see Foucault's view of history. History is essential to social theory. Critique is possible only at a distance. Critique employs the concrete descriptions of another time in order to describe the structures of social regulation. And, conversely, these histories describing the past provide the content for a critical understanding of the present. The history of madness calls modern psychiatry into question.[35] The history of the human sciences ends with a critique of the time of man.[36] A history of the prison was prompted by prison riots in France in 1972 and serves to critique the carceral system of the present.[37] Foucault's history is a critical social theory. "It establishes that we are difference, that our reason is the difference of discourses, our history the difference of times, ourselves the difference of masks. That difference, far from being the forgotten recovered origin, is the dispersion that we are and make."[38]

The statement and the archive are elements in the historian's world. They are technical. But they resist formalization by their placement in the overcast area between the visible and the hidden. On either side there are positivities. If specific practices form the visible limit of the statement, then archaeological descriptions of discursive formations are the reconstructed visibility of the force relations of a bellicose history. The regulatory field, invisible to the naked eye, is presented in historians' descriptions of discursive and social relations. Foucault's discursive formation, strangely marginal to the Marxian idea of social formation, is a system of rules. If practices are specific to readable statements in documents, then the discursive formation is specific to the regulatory discourse of the historian's descriptions. "To define a system of formation in its specific individuality is therefore to characterize a discourse or a group of statements by the regularity of a practice."[39] We return, hereby, to the semantic play between the rule and the regular. The rules which govern practices are discovered in the regularities described by the historian. And, again, history is social theory. Rules are laid bare by a positive history of the regular which history is the history of the discursive field. "This field is made up of the totality of all effective statements (whether spoken or written), in their dispersion as events and in the occurrence that is proper to them."[40]

The regulatory field is alternatively defined by the concept *discursive formation*, the events dispersed throughout a social formation, existing in a variety of series (the epistemological, the medical, the political, the economic, and so forth).

Whenever one can describe, between a number of statements, such a system of dispersion, whenever, between objects, one can define a regularity (an order, correlations, positions and functionings, transformations), we will say, for the sake of convenience, that we are dealing with a *discursive formation*—thus avoiding words that are already overladen with conditions and consequences, and in any case inadequate to the task of designating such a dispersion, such as "science," "Ideology," "theory," "domain of objectivity." The conditions to which the elements of this division (objects, mode of statement, concepts, thematic choices) are subjected we shall call the *rules of formation*. The rules of formation are conditions of existence (but also of coexistence, maintenance, modification and disappearance) in a given discursive division.[41]

It is, however, with discursive formation that one reaches the limits of *Archaeology of Knowledge*'s value for an understanding of Foucault's method. We have so far left uncontested a fundamental ambiguity in this book. What, precisely, is the relationship between discursive formation and social formation? We know that Foucault does not think society is nothing but discourse. We know also that the emphasis on discourse is a consequence of his attempt to revise social history. This much is clear. What we are not told, in so many words, is where discourse ends and society begins. We know there is a remainder after discourse. Discursive relations are "at the limit of discourse."[42] But what is on the other side of the boundary? Methodologically, we know that it is a space, empty but for the historians' translucent and opaque tools, statement and archive. But upon what does the historian gaze, beyond discourse? Is it, after discourse, the sheerness of "order in its primary state," as he said in *The Order of Things*. Not likely. Foucault suggests that the very idea of order as such, along with the master concept episteme, which implied that *The Order of Things* was organized around cultural totalities, was a mistake.[43] We know also that outside *Archaeology* he does not confine himself to discourse, even though it remains central. And within it, he clearly allows for primary relations "between institutions, techniques, social forms, etc.,"[44] which are not discursive. We are left with weak answers. Perhaps, because *The Archaeology of Knowledge* deals with knowledge, discursive relations are sufficient. Knowledge is found largely in texts, documents, books. Perhaps we can excuse the oversight by the fact that it was only after *Archaeology* that he clarified the intimacy of power and knowledge and went beyond the early view that power in knowledge simply controlled and excluded discourse.

We can, without embarrassment, leave *Archaeology* at this limit. It is simply a specific study bearing on knowledge. Most of its vocabulary disappears thereafter. What is essential to it for the question of Foucault's method is what is found elsewhere.[45] History works between practices and rules. Discourse is basic because, for the historian, this is where power and knowledge are joined.

3. Substance / POWER-KNOWLEDGE AND DISCOURSE

FOUCAULT'S HISTORICAL studies are attempts to understand contemporary social conflicts in terms of the economic, social, political, and epistemological conditions that led to their emergence. As such, they are not simply history, but philosophy and politics as well. Since he wants to escape traditional disciplinary classifications, yet include the concerns of history, philosophy, and politics, Foucault describes his method by the more illusive and general terms, genealogy and archaeology.

Genealogy or archaeology, for Foucault, is history defined by problems that are, at once, political and epistemological, or, better put, problems of power and knowledge. Thus the topics of his historical research—madness, clinical medicine, the human sciences, penality, sexuality—are problems that must be considered across the traditional disciplines and confined to no single one. Each concerns the rise of modern knowledge, most especially the social or human sciences. And each pertains to knowledge's relationship to power. Psychology, clinical medicine, the human sciences, criminology, population theory, political economy, modern biology, psychoanalysis and modern psychiatry are, each, implicated in modern society's attempt to shape and control persons. Each, therefore, requires critical reflection, simultaneously, on knowledge and politics.

It could be said, therefore, that Foucault's archaeology occupies an interstitial space between history, philosophy, and politics. This is, in effect, the same space as that, described in chapter 2, behind the methodological intersection of fact and the production of knowledge. Methodologically, fact and the production of knowledge form a site for historical work. Substantively (to use a term Foucault would not) philosophy and history are similarly joined at the point of political problems. "Philosophy's question therefore is the question as to what we ourselves are. That is why contemporary philosophy is entirely political and entirely historical. It is the politics immanent in history and the history indispensable for politics."[1] In short, the traditional distinction between method and substance in social science is eradicated. Fact and knowledge, philosophy and history, method and substance are relations poised around the visible conflicts of politics.

What contents are found in the space that history, philosophy, and politics create when, in overlapping, they fail to coincide? "Two words sum up everything: power and knowledge."[2] Though Foucault does not reduce everything to power and knowledge, the problems posed by the juxtaposition of these two topics provide the theoretical content to all of Foucault's writings, from *Madness and Civilization* to *The History of Sexuality*. If these problems are not defined with equal clarity in each work, especially at the beginning, they are present nonetheless throughout. Even *Madness and Civilization*, for example, deals with the way in which the economic, political, and moral factors involved in the confinement of unreason in the seventeenth and eighteenth centuries gradually isolated madness from unreason and turned it into subjectivity and psychological disease. To be sure, practices of moral discipline and medicine in confinement are not yet related to discourse and disciplinary codes. But the effects of power and knowledge are present in the history of madness, even though they are not fully articulated and examined.

Foucault is aware of this ambiguity. He has spoken of it many times. He is not embarrassed to admit that his inability in his early works to pose clearly the question of power and knowledge was partly due to the political malaise of the years during which they were written. Nor is he afraid to admit that his later works are a response to a changing political situation. The question of the mechanics of power could only be posed after 1968, with all that year represented for politics in France.[3] Similarly, 1972 is another watershed in the development of the question of power and knowledge. Foucault's researches into the history of penality and his experience at Attica prison led to a reformulation of the effects of power. Power, thereafter, is not merely negative, repressive, and prohibiting, but positive and productive, and explicitly bound to knowledge.[4]

Here the archaeological, more than the genealogical, image is useful. History, philosophy, and politics are historically active strata which divide and separate to form a three-dimensional volume. The subterranean cavern thus created is an open historical space in which power and knowledge are dispersed, resonating with each other and the three enclosing strata which, in turn, shift over time in relation to each other. Foucault works in this archaeological space in which the questions asked by history, philosophy, and politics themselves form the volume within which the dispersed, relational contents provide the specific materials of historical research. Power-knowledge, as the events of history, are defined by the regulating questions of the historian, who must also be philosopher and politician. Method and substance, we repeat, cannot be divorced. Thus, Foucault must take risks on several sides. While, on the one hand, he contends with the question of the meaning of history, he must, on the other hand, constantly expose himself to the uncertainties of his own language, the means by which that history is reconstructed.

The constructed concepts of the historian's discourse cannot be separated from the events on which he works. Thus, power-knowledge is not a formal, abstract tool so much as it is a theoretical weapon for struggling with these uncertainties. When power is joined to knowledge, then historical knowledge (*connaissance*) no less than knowledge (*savoir*) in history is called into question. This, once again, is why it is foolhardy to take Foucault's *Archaeology of Knowledge* more seriously than his substantive studies. It is in these concrete investigations that Foucault shapes historical knowledge by the examination of the play of knowledge (*savoir*) with power (*pouvoir*). Whatever the deficiencies in his explicit theory of power, Foucault, in each of his books, has been uncompromising in the insistence that power and knowledge are fused in the practices that comprise history. Madness is confined and made an object of moral discipline in *Madness and Civilization*. Through pathological anatomy the body, the seat of labor power, becomes visible as the seat of disease in *Birth of the Clinic*. Man appears through the concepts of life, labor, and language in *The Order of Things*. The disciplinary codes of incarceration give rise to a knowledge of the individual in *Discipline and Punish*. The prohibition of sex becomes the knowledge of sexuality in *The History of Sexuality*.

Without the exercise of power, knowledge would be left undefined, amorphous, and without any hold upon objectivity. Knowledge, for Foucault, is successively described as a political anatomy, a political economy, a discursive formation, a discursive disposition, and a political technology. Repressions and prohibitions, exclusions and rejections, techniques and methods bring individuals under surveillance. A clinical will to know (*libido sciendi*), which is nurtured in its cognitive operations is the exercise of power that practices subjection by the specification of objects and the creation of a domain of objectivity. To know is to exercise the power of subjection and domination; hence, power-knowledge.

THE ELLIPSIS OF DISCOURSE.   Foucault's history is also preoccupied with discourse. This preoccupation begins decisively with *The Birth of the Clinic*, where the birth of clinical medicine is described as the transformation of a set of concepts and practices that are uncovered by means of an analysis of discourse. Here Foucault's use of discourse to pinpoint discontinuous changes in medical practice introduces the distinction between epistemic knowledge (*savoir*) and accumulated knowledge (*connaissance*). Clinical medicine arose at the beginning of the nineteenth century by means of pathological anatomy and physiology, not by means of the continuous maturation of procedures and findings. Pathological anatomy and physiology introduce into the field of medical practices new discursive systems. Medicine changed because the rules for the formation of its statements underwent a transformation.

It is important to note that, even in his early writings. historical exposition depends upon discourse and its practice. *Madness and Civilization*, it is true, has little to say about discursive practices and almost nothing to say about historical methodology. But, even here, discourse is central, though silent, at the point where knowledge (*savoir*) must be disentangled from the matrix of social, economic, political, and institutional practices that surround it. Foucault's theory of discursive formations makes it possible to write the history of knowledge as the incorporation of those practices into discourse. There is a deliberate circularity here. However, this circularity does not reduce knowledge to a material substratum or to economic determination in the last instance. The point is that the materiality of discourse itself and the rules determining the formation of statements involve what, in *The Birth of the Clinic*, Foucault termed tertiary spatialization: "A system of options that reveals the way in which a group, in order to protect itself, practices exclusion, establishes the forms of assistance, and reacts to poverty and the fear of death."[5] *Discourse on Language* uses a different term, restrictive limitations; *The Archaeology of Knowledge* discusses the same problem under the title of discursive modalities.

The concept of a discursive formation, a system of statements, makes it possible to distinguish epistemic knowledge (*savoir*) from accumulated knowledge (*connaissance*). Simultaneously, it exposes the work of power in knowledge. In *The Birth of the Clinic*, where Foucault first begins to develop the idea power-knowledge, the medical gaze is structured not only by means of discourse, but also by the social relations in which it is embedded. The social relations of subjection and domination are, however, incorporated into clinical perception by discourse: the semiotics of the sign behind the reading of symptoms, the language into which young practitioners must be initiated, the anticipation of the invisible anatomy of the corpse onto the surface visibility of the living body, the transgression of taboo in the *libido sciendi* at work in the new use of palpation in the nineteenth century. Even the theory of discursive systems in *The Archaeology of Knowledge*, with its attendant concepts of discursive practice, episteme, and archive, involves, implicitly, the juncture of power and knowledge in discourse.

But discourse is only a juncture, a point at which knowledge and power meet. Discourse is not everything. Foucault is not developing a new theory of discourse in the vein of hermeneutic philosophy in France (Ricoeur) or Germany (Gadamer). In fact, after *The Archaeology of Knowledge* discourse recedes into the background. *Discipline and Punish* focuses on the semio-techniques of power in the practices of incarceration; *The History of Sexuality*, on bio-power, power over the processes of life, in the knowledge of sexuality. *The Archaeology of Knowledge* is more an interruption than a decisive event in the development of Foucault's problematic. The goal of Foucault's works is not to create a new semiology in which social, economic, and political relations are explained as discursive relations.

The theory of discourse is a starting point of which, as his work takes shape, he has less need. But begin he must; hence the prominence, for a time, of the obstructive materiality of discursive practices. "I am supposing," Foucault writes in *Discourse on Language*, "that in every society the production of discourse is at once controlled, selected, organized and redistributed according to a certain number of procedures, whose role is to avert its powers and its dangers, to cope with chance events, to evade its ponderous, awesome materiality."[6] There are rules of exclusion: prohibitions, rejections, and divisions;

restrictive limitations on the exercise of discourse: rituals, fellowships of discourse, and doctrines; internal limitations upon discourse: commentaries, authors, and disciplines.[7] These operations in the construction of discursive practices are concealed behind a number of philosophical themes dominant in Western thought: the founding subject, experience as origin, and universal mediation. What is concealed in these concepts and operations? Are they not merely impurities that affect ideal truth in its passage to the concrete? Are not the distortions of discourse the marks of the historical contingency of truth? Do not these distortions leave untouched the conception of truth as ideal, as the telos of all human discourse, and the ultimate ground of all knowledge?

For Foucault, the possibility of asking these questions is an indication that these distortions have produced a will to truth distinct from desire and power. The dangers and risks of discourse are concealed in the concept of true discourse. Discourse, animated by the will to truth, is a form of dissemblance. The will to truth distorts itself in order to reappear in the guise of ideal truth. In their dialectic, true discourse and the will to truth conceal the truth. "True discourse, liberated by the nature of its form from desire and power, is incapable of recognizing the will to truth which pervades it; and the will to truth, having imposed itself upon us for so long, is such that the truth it seeks to reveal cannot fail to mask it."[8] Foucault's theory of discourse, therefore, involves violence and transgression. An original transgression: the concealment of the will to truth in the ideal of true discourse. A secondary transgression: the concealment of the will to truth in the very concept of truth. A third transgression: the violence done to the taboos erected in the first two transgressions by "the political history of the production of 'truth.'"[9] Discourse, power, and knowledge involve a history of transgressions.

TRANSGRESSION.   True discourse only surfaces in a form twisted by violence. The face it turns toward men, "wealth, fertility and sweet strength in all of its insidious universality,"[10] is the calm exterior visage of power. The domineering free gaze of the clinic is matched by the cold, calculating gaze inhabiting Bentham's panopticon. The reverse side of the liberation of truth is the subjection of all to its gaze. Subjection and freedom intermingle. Power-knowledge is originally a violence done to the truth in which truth appears as ideal, original, and innocent. Transgression takes the form of knowledge and power.

It is possible to expand this circularity of transgressions and use the will to truth against itself? Is it possible to unmask the concealments, elisions, productive prohibitions, positive repressions, which are the political technology of power-knowledge? Archaeology, or what, after *The Archaeology of Knowledge*, Foucault calls genealogy, is the transgressive knowledge in which the taboos thrown up around the will to truth are violated. The genealogy of knowledge transgresses the divisions of the true and the false, reason and madness, by the attempt "to remould this will to truth and to turn it against truth at that very point where truth undertakes to justify the taboo, and to define madness."[11] Nietzsche, Bataille, and Artaud are the sentinels that guard the bridges over which the dialectic of transgression passes. The concept power-knowledge is the result.

Thus, the critical theory announced in Foucault's Collège de France inaugural address, *Discourse on Language*, becomes quite explicit in subsequent studies. History, unmistakably, is a critical exposition of the constitution of knowledge through the techniques of power. In *Discipline and Punish* Foucault unmasks the power over and knowledge of individuals in the semio-techniques of disciplinary codes. In *The History of Sexuality* he discloses the control over human populations and the objectification of self-consciousness at work in bio-power. Foucault's history is a critical analysis of the socially contingent nature of truth gained by crossing the divide between the true and the false. The historical reality of the will to truth is its complicity with power and not its neutrality or freedom from evaluative judgments. Every conception of ideal truth, including the dream of value neutrality in the social sciences, is a falsification of the operations of true discourse. Ideal truth does not liberate discourse from power, but tightens power's control. The taboo under which power and knowledge are placed reinforces an oppression made more effective because it cannot be criticized.

History is a critique of truth's distortion. But, equally, history is produced by transgressing a taboo that can never, finally, be criticized. History's truth is immanent, not transcendental. As such it must struggle, without hope of pure freedom, against the primal fact of all truth, distortion. Power-knowledge, remember, involves three transgressions. In the first two the will to truth is hidden behind discourse and truth itself. In the third, the historian, in a political act, overcomes the concrete taboos by which truth is hidden. But the taboo cannot be removed. It is reinforced in transgression. As a result, critical knowledge is not, for Foucault, the restoration of a primeval innocence or a primitive originality in which one can look upon the visage of truth without a veil. The "history of the production of truth" is not a return to an original peace free of violence or repression. Transgression, for Foucault, entails no pristine true discourse. Transgression is an original feature of the will to knowledge. It is also a feature of the recounting of its history. Transgression is the eternal return of the truth upon itself, a primitive circularity in which distorted truth only meets up once again with distorted truth. Here is Nietzsche's Eternal Return of the Same. The history of the production of truth is thus not a perspective outside of the circularity of knowledge, but the worm hidden in the breast of truth.

In the concept of transgression, Foucault's relation to Bataille is evident. But Foucault does not give to transgression the same positive significance that the term had for Bataille. For Bataille, in *Death and Sensuality*, humanity has placed upon sexuality a primitive taboo. The knowledge of life, then, was the violent act of crossing that barrier. However, in spite of the critiques that have suggested there is an unspoken naturalism in Foucault's writings, particularly in his earlier works, *Madness and Civilization* and *The Birth of the Clinic*, transgression for him does not entail the hypothesis of an original state. The will to truth exists as a transgression upon its ideal possibilities.

All of this takes place within language. In the effort to speak, the Subject does not encounter within himself an irreducible center of certainty, but a contest thrown up by the limits of his being and the void created by the death of God, the ultimate representation of limit. In language the Subject is up against his own finitude and the fact that he is stripped of transcendence.[12] In a post-Sadean language, the concept of transgression says that meaning is confronted not as an absolute transcendence grounding language, but in the limits of meaning. Language is the existence of sense in the recognition of limits defined by "the limit of the Limitless."[13] But sense is not created by remaining within limits, such as the analytic of finitude, as if they constituted a new set of positivities within which humanity is reconstituted. Sense is, rather, in the excess that transgresses those limits.

For Bataille, eroticism arises when sexuality crosses the limits erected by the taboo on sexuality. Eroticism both crosses and sustains the limit of the taboo. The limit is an internal necessity for transgression. At the same time, it is the recognition that, in crossing the limit, the taboo is not eliminated. Transgression is the movement that creates, in the absence of an absolute Limit, a limitlessness essential to the transgression of limits. The dialectic is engendered by its own internal elements. But, then, this is no longer a dialectic. Language at this point is nondiscursive. It is neither positive, nor negative, because it neither affirms, nor denies division, separation, or distance. Language recognizes only the "existence of difference."[14] The language of transgression confronts and interrogates limits. Contestation occurs without resolution; hence, "the Nietzschean figures of tragedy, of Dionysus, of the death of God, of the philosopher's hammer, of the Superman [Overman] approaching with the steps of a dove, of the Return."[15]

The language of transgression must be distinguished from the analytic of finitude described in *The Order of Things*. The finite in the language of transgression does not rest upon the positivity of finitude. In contrast, the analytic of Man's finitude, rejected by Foucault, is basic to Man as an object of knowledge in the social sciences. The nineteenth century analytic is founded upon a field of positive data, the data of life, labor, and language. Man's finitude is the limit drawn by the recognition of the factual character of his existence. This finitude is determined by ontic regions, life, labor, and language, in the knowledge of which Man can be grasped. Whether it is "the anatomy of the brain, the mechanics of production costs, or the system of Indo-European conjugation,"[16] life, labor, and language define what is possible and impossible for men. These positive regions not only determine the finite limits of Man, but are the expression of his finitude. They are positivities formed from the limits of "the spatiality of the body, the yawning of desire, and the time of language."[17] Man's finitude mirrors the finite content of the areas of knowledge through which he is known. The limits in the analytic of finitude are positive limits within which Man appears as an object of knowledge.

Transgressive knowledge, by contrast, is not a knowledge of finitude, nor an anthropological thought that in the absence of God has Man as its epistemological center.[18] The absence or death of God is, for Foucault as it was with Nietzsche, the rejection of the theological nature of Western thought. Transgressive thought does not presuppose an ontic ground for the divisions of reason and madness, the true and the false. For Foucault, transgression does not signify a thought that determines limits, as if what can be known about man contains, a priori, all the limits to be placed upon his existence. An a priori knowledge of human finitude does not result in a determination of the epistemological limits of man's knowledge. Transgressive thought is as far from philosophical anthropology as it is from theology. Transgression represents "the still silent and groping apparition of a form of thought in which the interrogation of the limit replaces the search for totality and the act of transgression replaces the movement of contradictions."[19]

The terms limit, excess, and transgression appear, mostly, in Foucault's philosophical texts, but the concepts are essential to a reading of his historical studies. From *Madness and Civilization* to *The History of Sexuality* Foucault analyzes the limits placed upon reason and madness, the true and the false, by tracing the history within which those limits were constituted. The division of reason and madness appears first in the political and economic crises surrounding the rise and dissolution of confinement in the seventeenth and eighteenth centuries and the isolation of madness within the empirical forms of unreason by means of bourgeois social order. The division is completed in the moralization of madness effected through the moral therapeutics practiced in the asylums of Tuke and Pinel. With *The Birth of the Clinic* the claim of the clinical gaze to be the recovery of original experience is shattered. Foucault relativizes this privileged limit by means of a history of the dispersed events that constituted the clinic: the founding of the French Royal Society of Medicine, the control of epidemics, the financing of hospitals, the practices of pathological anatomy, the liberalization of medical perception in the transgression of modesty in the examination of women, and the conceptualization of the medical gaze as a field of free economic exchange. In *The Order of Things*, the history of the human sciences as a chronicle of accumulated knowledge is dissolved into a history of the discursive systems in which science arises in knowledge, *savoir*. The appearance of Man as an object of the social sciences is not the triumphant achievement of a scientific methodology, but is due to the sudden appearance of a configuration of the concepts life, labor, and language in the nineteenth century.

The knowledge of individuals gained through the localization of disease in the visible body and knowledge of the individual body arising through pathological anatomy is extended in *Discipline and Punish*. The penal practices born through the penal reforms of the seventeenth and eighteenth centuries lead, not to rehabilitation, but to a micro-power invested in disciplines borrowed from the penitential practices of individual confession, the pedagogy of the Christian schools of the nineteenth century, the political ideology of the open republic. All are symbolized in the universally dominant case of Bentham's panopticon. The penal practices of the eighteenth and nineteenth centuries spawned a series of individualizing disciplines in which the prisoner is isolated and his behavior fragmented. As semio-techniques, they signify the individual in his specificity. The individual is thrown back into a self-conscious remorse. Through the practices of incarceration and attendant judicial measures, the seizure of the individual as the object of knowledge accompanies a normalization of reason. Reason is the norm. By means of the extension of carceral disciplines, society at large comes under the discipline of the rational norm. In *The History of Sexuality*, the myth of Victorian repression hides the true function of the discourse of sexuality. That function is not liberation, but the creation of a discourse able to dispose of sex in such a way that sexuality is the manifestation of social control and power over life.

Reason, from *Madness and Civilization* to *The History of Sexuality*, is found in the strategies, disciplines, technologies, and tactics which power exercises on the body. In that fundamental fact, there is a transgression on the divisions that constitute the macro-history and the macro-power of rationality: madness and reason, the true and the false, body and soul, the individual and society, power and knowledge, words and things, the confined and the free, repression and liberation, politics and transcendent religion, the state and the family, life and death. Having transgressed its own nature, reason placidly aligns itself with one side or another of the dichotomies it has given rise to by its violence. The history that transgresses these divisions is a micro-history that discloses the small, dirty details of mechanisms dispersed throughout the social body, and installed here and there in institutions; mechanisms that create a schedule and spatial order for bodily actions.

THE FRACTURED BODY.   Where is this history located? It is in economic history, but a history not exhausted by the multiple transgressions of exchange. It is in political history, yet one not confined to the confrontation of classes. It is in social history, nevertheless, not one found in the rise and death of institutions. It is in intellectual history, but not a history for which ideas are the original signs of reality. Foucault's history is not traditional. It is located where knowledge has the body in its grip; where, in the time and space of the body, relations of power pinpoint a field of objectivity. How do events produce effects? How is history effective so that it can trace the "descent" and the "emergence" of cultural acquisitions, economic attitudes, political dispositions, and moral values? How is it possible for the ruptures, reversals, discontinuities, and transformations located in a series of events to possess materiality?

To familiar questions, Foucault gives a single, unfamiliar answer: because events are inscribed upon the body. The inscribed body is the space wherein the Hydra of history can look in all directions simultaneously. Foucault, however, does not develop a philosophy of the body in which history would take on flesh as it did for Merleau-Ponty. The inscribed body is the correlate of the concept of genealogy. "Genealogy, as an analysis of descent, is thus situated within the articulation of the body and history. Its task is to expose a body totally imprinted by history and the process of history's destruction of the body."[20]

The body is the space in which it is possible to find, not the traces of past events, but the play of forces in which the surface events of history are distortions of "lost events."[21] Foucault is following Nietzsche very closely here. "Descent" and "emergence" are Nietzsche's *Herkunft* and *Entstehung*. But the tapestry woven from those terms is Foucault's. The descent or emergence of an idea, a trait or characteristic, a social discipline, or rational conception, is the manner in which they are events subject to the reversals, discontinuities, forces of domination, risks and wagers, accidents and chances in which every event is caught. The body is inscribed with the play of creation and destruction, or risks and wagers, in which there is the reality of loss and not the forgotten plenitude of sensible meaning. The body is not the land flowing with milk and honey, but the plain of desolation, the desert in which history wanders.

The Birth of the Clinic is Foucault's first obvious history of the body. The clinical gaze is inscribed in an epistemic field constituted by the placement of death within the organs of the living body by pathological anatomy. The body is the field of objectivity in which the visibility of the body is known through its invisibility, the anticipated inner space of the body revealed to vision by autopsy. Beginning with Bichat, life is defined by death. Disease is a possibility installed in life, its contrary. The truth of disease is revealed in death. Life and the living body are only known against the backdrop of death. The body is also the space traversed in transgressing the shame involved in the palpation of the unclothed body. That transgression of modesty is the action of a *libido sciendi*, a desire to know whose manifest form is an encroachment upon bodily space.

The clinic is born in a gaze whose domain is the threat of destruction leveled against the living body. The clinic necessarily entails death and transgression. The medical gaze locates and individualizes disease in the body by holding the body in subjection. For the clinical gaze to know is for it to dominate the bodies of those condemned to death and poverty. The clinic's ability to locate disease in the body is made possible by the poor, who, with their bodies, pay an interest on capital advanced in the hospitals financed by the rich after the

Revolution. The poor exchange their bodies for medical care. Clinical knowledge of diseases occurs by means of the political subjection that opens up the body to the clinical gaze.

Madness is also constituted in the domination of the body. Madness as a mental disease arises from the practice of confining bodies in the eighteenth century. *Madness and Civilization* focuses on the isolation of madness from the generality of unreason by the intervention of the moral law in confinement and through the construction of asylums in which madness became a subjectivity through the experience of moral guilt. The mad are confined as the consequence of a moral perception. Madness, sloth, and poverty intermingle. The body of unreason is distinguished from the body of labor. In confinement, madness is isolated by breaking the classical unity of the soul and the body. The unity of unreason is broken by viewing madness as a state of animality inhabited by the frenzy of an unchained freedom, and, in the therapeutics of madness, by associating madness with delirium and dissociating it from passion, the untrammeled desire of the body. The moralization of madness in the rise of the asylums creates the moral subjectivity of madness against the background of a fractured body. Likewise, reason is separated from unreason by separating the soul from the body. The body is dismembered to produce a soul which has its existence in the movements of a delirious language tortured by the guilt produced by moral punishment. Subjectivity is the object of psychological observation and knowledge. Subjectivity, thereby, comes into existence by the subjection of the body in confinement. It is the internalization of moral subjection in the asylum. In the history of madness, the subjectivity of madness is the result of the subjection of the body. The body in subjection is the site in which emerges the field of objectivity that psychology will claim as its own.

In *Discipline and Punish*, Foucault confronts knowledge (*savoir*) with the epistemological technology that defines its object, the semio-techniques of disciplinary codes. Here, quite explicitly, is the body "totally imprinted by history and the process of history's destruction of the body." The body in *Discipline and Punish* is the fractured body, inscribed with a multiplicity of individuating and objectifying techniques. The initial scene with which *Discipline and Punish* begins is the execution of Damiens. His body is tortured by pincers and quartered. The four horses are unable to separate his limbs from his trunk. He must be hacked apart. This fragmentation is a sign of sovereign, unlimited power. At the end of *Discipline and Punish* the body is subjected to the panoptic gaze and to the regime of isolation. It is thrown back on its own conscience to produce a new morality. Its movements through the day and night of the prison are ordered according to a rigorous schedule. Movements are subjected to the discipline of labor. In brief, the body is now cut into a soul and physical body and dispersed among the fragments of mechanical time. The fractured body inscribed with the history of penal institutions and their discipline is caught up in a continuous movement of desynthesization.

In the distance between these two images of the body Foucault writes the history of punishment and prisons. The distance is traversed by a "political technology of the body." What is Foucault's aim in writing *Discipline and Punish*? One sentence spells it out: "In short, try to study the metamorphosis of punitive methods on the basis of a political technology of the body in which might be read a common history of power relations and object relations."[22] Foucault's problem in *Discipline and Punish* is the rise of the prison to dominate the field of penal punishment and the means used to create the disciplinary codes of the prison, the school, military life, and religious practice. This historical problem requires the exposition of the relations of power and knowledge and the formulation of the concept power-knowledge. In turn, such a theoretical formulation involves the description of the ways that power and knowledge are inscribed upon the body. Inscription, thus, is a political technology of the body in which cognitive relations are the exercise of power and power relations are objectifying.

The fracturing of the body not only corresponds to the fragmentation of the body in disciplinary codes, it also corresponds to the dispersion of power relations. Foucault views power not as a privilege to be defended, but as a contract governing exchange. The model Foucault prefers is that of a "network of relations, constantly in tension" and "a perpetual battle."[23] The rise of the prison as a dominant form of judicial punishment in the eighteenth and nineteenth centuries is not an isolated event. The discipline of the body introduced by the prison gathers together disciplinary codes originating at different points in society. The confrontation of power and knowledge comes to a head in the history of penality because penal practices pervade society. Disciplinary codes are a "microphysics of power," the crucial nature of which is that they are a *strategy*. Power is not privilege, but strategy. Its dispersion within the social body is direct evidence for the process that associated the accumulation of capital in the West with the accumulation of men.[24] The accumulation of capital is accompanied by strategies for marshalling the productive force of the body, intensifying its productivity by disciplining its movements. The economic use of the body is related to the political use of the body. As labor power disciplined for productivity, the body is also need, calculatedly nurtured in subjection. The body is politicized. "But the body is also directly involved in a political field; power relations have an immediate hold upon it, they invest it, mask it, train it, torture it, force it to carry out tasks, to perform ceremonies, to emit signs."[25]

This political technology of the body is also a strategy and technique for delimiting the natural movements of the body: "there may be a 'knowledge' of the body that is not exactly the science of its functioning, and a mastery of its forces that is more than the ability to conquer them: this knowledge and this mastery constitute what might be called the political technology of the body."[26] This knowledge surfaces in military manuals, which translate the natural movements of the body into the most precise and efficient drills. It is the knowledge formulated in the Christian schools of La Salle, in which the body is subjected to the regime of pedagogy. It is a knowledge that produces a docile body, taught by turning its own forces against itself. This knowledge is a power. It intensifies the efficiency and productivity of the body.

Discipline and Punish, therefore, is a study of political anatomy. The material support for the relations of power and knowledge in society is the body politic. The political anatomy of society is the political economy of the body. Both images involve a set of correspondences and transferences that define the strategies inscribed upon the body as the social strategies by which power works. The body politic is "a set of material elements and techniques that serve as weapons, relays, communication routes, and supports for the power and knowledge relations that invest human bodies and subjugate them by turning them into objects of knowledge."[27] The fractured and subjected body of penal practices is the body in a political field in which power is exercised in society. Damiens' body was drawn to the four quarters of the earth. The docile body of penal practices and disciplinary codes is pulverized into a multiplicity of details, directions, attitudes, and postures anchored in the body of society. The exercise of the microphysics of power on the docile body is its dispersion, its fragmentation into its internal parts that, left intact, produce a living division within the body.

One of the principal effects of the body's division is the doubling of the imprisoned body into the soul. The soul as it is encountered in the extrajudicial, administrative practices of penality in the eighteenth century and in the practices of the disciplinary codes of the eighteenth and nineteenth centuries is the result of the individuation of punishment. The individuation of punishment creates an object for the application of power in which consideration must be given to extenuating circumstances, intentions, psychological abnormality, and legal responsibility. In developing the application of punishment, the political technology of power effects an internalization of its own relations within the body of the imprisoned. If the surplus power of the king in the ancien régime gave rise to the duplication of his body in the body politic, then Foucault sees the surplus power exercised on the body of the condemned as giving rise to another kind of duplication, the soul. The genealogy of the modern soul has its roots in the microphysics of power.[28] The soul is not the metaphysical double of the body. Power turns the body against itself, divides it from itself into the imprisoned body and the soul in the throes of remorse.

Thus, where power and knowledge meet in the fragmenting of the body, the soul arises as the object of knowledge and as the subject of individuation. "It would be wrong," Foucault writes in *Discipline and Punish*, "to say that the soul is an illusion, or an ideological effect. On the contrary, it exists, it has a reality, it is produced permanently around, on, within the body by the functioning of a power that is exercised on those punished—and, in a more general way, on those one supervises, trains, and corrects, over madmen, children at home and at school, the colonized, over those who are stuck at a machine and supervised for the rest of their lives."[29] This psychological complex of power and knowledge is not simply the field of the concepts of psyche, personality, subjectivity, and consciousness. It is also the reference for the construction of the psychological sciences. They, and their field of objectivity, the soul, are the result of a "new political anatomy of the body."[30]

A political anatomy of the body is also a new political economy of desire. It is the former in *The Birth of the Clinic*, *Madness and Civilization*, and *Discipline and Punish*; the latter in *The History of Sexuality*. The body of desire in *The History of Sexuality* is the domain of a knowledge (*savoir*) that constitutes itself in the myth of repression in modern societies. In confronting the body of desire as *the* secret forbidden by the prohibition upon sexuality,[31] the will to know (*volonté de savoir*) is transformed into the discourse on sexuality for whom repression is merely an index of its proliferation throughout society. Shame was the limit transgressed in the desire to know (*libido sciendi*) when, in the nineteenth century, doctors dared to examine the visible body by touch. Likewise, repression is the myth transgressed by the will to know taking form in the discourse on sexuality. The desire to know is a form of knowledge in which to know life is also to control it; in which to know desire is also to shape it politically from within. Discourse on sexuality is a form of power-knowledge.

The emergence of the discourse of sexuality entails the appearance of a "new distribution of pleasures, types of discourses, truths, and kinds of powers."[32] This is the affective mechanism of sexuality (*dispositif de sexualité*), which, beginning with the eighteenth century, involves four strategies centered on four privileged objects: the hysterical woman, the masturbating child, the Malthusian couple, the adult pervert. To these objects four strategies: hystericalization of the body of the woman, the pedagogization of the sex of the child, the socialization of the procreative activities, and the psychiatrization of perverse pleasures.[33]

What is involved in these strategies? Nothing less than the production of the affective mechanism of sexuality itself, and the sexed body. Sexuality is not a repressed, hidden instinct, difficult to conceptualize. The discourse of sexuality produces the truth of the sexual body in such a manner that the desires of the flesh come to know themselves and are known as objects of knowledge (*savoir*). The affective mechanism of sexuality is the "great surface network in which the stimulation of bodies, the intensification of pleasures, the incitement to discourse, the formation of special knowledges, the strengthening of controls and resistances, are linked to one another in accordance with a few major strategies of knowledge and power."[34] The history of this sexuality is the history of the discourse in which the strategies of knowledge and power come to the surface.

What is at work in this shameless discourse that constantly reveals its own secrets? Above all, the masking of power in the myth of repression. Repression is represented as the imposition of an interdiction coming from the outside, an imposition of power external to the discourse of sexuality. Its model is the power of right (*pouvoir de droit*), liberation from which is the assertion of a corresponding right, the right of sexuality to be free. The liberation of sexuality is based on freeing sexuality from a "juridico-discursive" power in which, on one side, there is the legislating power and, on the other, the obedient subject.[35] It is, in fact, a game of the licit and the illicit, of transgression and punishment. The model of juridico-discursive power conceals a power that operates through the discourse of sexuality not in terms of law, but normalization; not in terms of right, but technique; not in terms of punishment, but control.[36] This power is the object of an analytic of power, rather than a theory of power. "The definition of the specific domain which relations of power form and the determination of the instruments which make it possible to analyse it."[37] In formulating the method appropriate to a history of sexuality, *The History of Sexuality* presents, at the same time, a critique of power as normalization, technique, and social control.

The sexual body is revealed as an effect of power and knowledge. *The History of Sexuality* analyzes the sexualization of the body as the production of a specific type of desire. The discourse of sexuality is a definite desire to know. The sexual body, therefore, is a specific form of desire in which subjectivity is produced. *Madness and Civilization* and *Discipline and Punish* dealt with the constitution of subjectivity in the confined and incarcerated body. *The History of Sexuality* plunges deeper into that morass by concentrating on the constitution of subjectivity in the self-consciousness of desire. If Hegel, in the *Phenomenology of the Spirit*, saw the formation of a dialectic in the birth of self-consciousness's desire for the other, then Foucault sees the analytic of power subjected to political critique.

The sexualization of the body is the effect of power in the discourse of sexuality. In particular, it is the discourse in which the rising bourgeois class creates for itself a distinctive relationship to sexuality. For the symbolic significance of blood, the bourgeoisie substitutes an analytic of sexuality. Where the traditional aristocracy relied on parentage, the bourgeoisie employed heredity, eugenics, and degeneration. Sex for the bourgeoisie is the autosexualization of its body in which it affirms itself by raising the political price of its body.[38] What differentiated the bourgeoisie from other classes was not the quality of it sexuality, but the intensity of its repression.[39] At the moment when programs were being launched to repress incest in the rural population, psychoanalysis was aiding the bourgeoisie to discover incest in the midst of family relationships and to liberate their incestuous desires. The price of repression is high, but affordable. The discourse of sexuality pays the price by proliferating a multitude of ways in which sexuality is tied to the value of life. The increase in the number of writings on health and long life attest to this coupling of the vigor of the body with political and economic hegemony. Here, for Foucault, is the social significance of repression.

The discourse of sexuality is not, therefore, a power exercised over other classes. It is a strategy in which the bourgeoisie develops its own sexuality first of all. The battle against sexual repression in the name of sexual freedom is part of the apparatus of repression. The theory of repression is part and parcel of the affective mechanism of sexuality. Repression is for the bourgeoisie a sign of the difference of its sexuality and sexualized body. The myth of repression is tied to the diffusion of the discourse of sexuality throughout the whole social body. In becoming generalized, in sexualizing the bodies of other classes, the myth of repression sets apart the bodies of the bourgeoisie. They are more repressed. The sexuality of the bourgeoisie is under a more intense interdict than is the sexuality of others. "Henceforth," Foucault writes, "social differentiation will be affirmed not by the 'sexual' quality of the body, but by the intensity of its repression."[40]

The analytic gaze of clinical medicine was made possible by the installation of death into the living, viable body; the power-knowledge of the discourse of sexuality is a prolongation of the monarchical power over life and death. For the monarch, the power over life is the power over death: "the right to put to death and let live."[41] This is juridico-discursive power. But, since the Classical Age and the ancien régime, the power to allow someone to live has taken the form of controlling life. In the Modern Age the power to put to death has been transformed into the power to make live, "a power that exerts a positive influence on life, that endeavors to administer, optimize, and multiply it, subjecting it to precise controls and comprehensive regulations."[42] This is bio-power, a politics in which the body is subject to the control of discipline and, as the subject of biological processes, to population controls.

In disciplinary controls, the body is viewed as a machine. In population controls, the body is the "mechanism of life" that can be channeled, increased, extended, and decreased. The body is the object of a political anatomy and of a bio-politics of population.[43] These are the two poles for the development of the power of life from which emerge the sexed body and the discourse of sexuality. In bio-power, the body, as the seat of biological processes, enters into history and knowledge as a specific domain. The important phenomenon taking place in social history with the beginning of capitalism was not the ascetic morality that disparaged the body, but the entrance into power-knowledge of biological processes as the object of political techniques.[44] The knowledge of the body is gained through a pulverization of the body, a dispersion of the body into a multiplicity of political strategies and techniques.

Sexuality is the truth of desire. In the politics of life the truth of man is in question. The anthropological view of man is equally a descendent of madness,[45] of the discourse of sexuality, and of the politics of life. Man comes to occupy a biological space in which desire is turned into self-knowledge and humanity is in question. In contrast to Aristotelean man, a living being with the capacity for political existence, modern man, for Foucault, is "an animal whose politics places his existence as a living being in question."[46] This biological space is where the truth of man appears, not only because history is surrounded by biological events, but because biological life has taken a place in history. Biological life is the interior truth of humanity. Here *The History of Sexuality* joins *Madness and Civilization* and *The Order of Things*. In contrast to the Classical Age, in which man was viewed in relationship to truth, the Modern Age views humanity as truth taking shape within itself. Hence, the madman, finitude, and biological life are the figures which characterize modernity. But *The History of Sexuality* adds an important qualification. Biological life is where humanity is turned back upon itself. Where it becomes true, on the basis of a history infused with the techniques of knowledge and power. The truth of humanity and the possibility of an anthropological view of man as a living being is born in the development of a bio-power and bio-politics.

The analyses of the discourse of sexuality in *The History of Sexuality* depend, therefore, on an analysis of power and knowledge: a knowledge of life and a power over life at the limits of death. The sexed body, sex, is born in the politics of the discipline of the body and the control of populations.[47] Sexuality is the meaning inscribed on the body by the politics of life. In the case of psychonanalysis, the discourse of sexuality is a dematerialization of the body. It is an effacement of the body in a politics of desire dominated by the figures of law, the prohibition of incest, the Father-Sovereign. But the politics of life does not destroy the body. Rather *The History of Sexuality* takes the body's effacement as its object. "In any case," Foucault writes of this book, "the goal of the present study is to show how the affective mechanisms of power are articulated directly upon the body—upon bodies, functions, physiological processes, sensations, and pleasures."[48] The body is not merely the field in which the game of power is played out. The desire for sex is the effect of the discourse of sexuality, a sexuality affected by the power over life.

Sex is not an autonomous function of the body corrupted by power. Sex is a knowledge of sexuality that uses the findings of the biological sciences to normalize sexual behavior. In normalizing the sexual behavior of the body, in creating a norm against which the body will measure itself, sex interjects within the body the residue of power. Sexual instinct, thereby, becomes a power opposed to power; hence a force that must be forbidden and repressed. This sex is not an autonomous biological force, an instinct inherent in the body, a dynamism of pure nature. Sex is a theory.[49] It is a speculative and ideal construction, the result of a discourse of sexuality embedded in the strategies and techniques of power. Sex is not the body in its most intimate and secret parts, but a discursive body, a fractured and divided body, a body whose inner articulation of desire is a political pulverization.

The history of the material body proposed in the first volume of *The History of Sexuality* would expose the facade of an autonomous, unified, and integral sex for what it is: the result of a history in which the body is fractured by power. As instinct and function, as the generation of goals and meanings, sexuality is first of all conceived on the model of perversion, fetishism. Fetishism serves as the basis for the analysis of other deviations and for the way in which the sexual instinct is related to its object. Sexuality is under the reign of the norm and the power of normalization. In addition, in the affective mechanism of sexuality, sex appears against the background cast by the four great figures of sexuality: hysteria, onanism, fetishism, and coitus interruptus. In its knowledge of its sexuality, the body is divided against itself. It is dispersed among a range of phenomena objectified in the discourse of sexuality. Thus, within the strategies of the affective mechanism of sexuality, sex appears as a series of divisions "of whole and part, principle and lack, absence and presence, excess and deficiency, by the function of instinct, finality, and meaning, of reality and pleasure."[50]

From *Madness and Civilization* to *The History of Sexuality* the body is cut to pieces and scattered over the field created by the strategies of political technology. The divided and fractured body is marked by the historical events of discourse, of power-knowledge, of politics, and of class struggle. Foucault's history, thereby, is material, not incarnational. The figure of Damiens at the beginning of *Discipline and Punish*, his flesh ripped by pincers and finally hacked apart, is, in a sense, an *Urleib*, a proto-Body, but not as the primeval source of all the meanings lived in the conscious experience of the social body. Damiens' body is the *Urleib* of politics in which anthropological and psychological man appeared. The soul and the consciousness of modern man are the dematerialization of the bodies of the madman, the sick, the imprisoned, and the repressed. But, even more, this body is also used like so many cobblestones to erect a barricade against death.

POLITICS AND DEATH. Power does not deal with death by repressing the consciousness of death, but by constructing a dialogue with death in which life is the object of power and knowledge. The two, power and death, belong together for Foucault, just as writing and death belong together for Blanchot, and death and sensuality for Bataille. The space in which consciousness and language can turn back over themselves and against death is a doubled space thrown up against death: the constant play of setting up limits and transgressing them, the play of mirrors at the heart of consciousness in which consciousness finds security in seeing itself seeing itself to infinity. Power-knowledge is the objectification of the body within the limits established by strategies. Is it not a technology whose inner passion is to indefinitely stave off the fatal sentence of death?

Death has a place in Foucault's writings because his historical analyses are political. Foucault's history charts the divisions, caesuras, reversals, and changes that are the specific configurations of power and knowledge. Politics involves a dialogue with death because death divides and fractures the body. Politics is not a tender caress that plays over the surface of the body. It disciplines and punishes the body, breaks it down into its parts in order to turn its natural forces into the instruments of its bondage. Politics installs death within the very core of the body's visibility, so that the truth of its visible surface is the black night of the corpse. Politics maintains power over life by transforming death into its private secret, suicide, and it infuses the body with a sexuality worth the price of death. The power and knowledge that politics uses are the horrifying images of death in history. And it is the transgression of the limits within which the circularity of language and consciousness makes possible, in history, a critical discourse by which the strategies and objectifications of power-knowledge can be analyzed.

Death is not an experience. It is an absence, a void. There is no reflection that can indirectly or directly discover signs of its plenitude, of its full presence. Without that discovery, death can never be an object of thought. To be face to face with death is not to be confronted with another visage. Death is the exterior space, the dissimulating time, in which subjectivity and the self cannot rejoin themselves in self-consciousness and self-knowledge. Death is not their object. Subjectivity and the self are not mirrored in death. Death is the disruption of the circularity of the self and subjectivity in the yawning of an uncloseable rupture. To be face to face with death is for subjectivity to be dispersed into an indefinite space. Death is the absence of totality and plenitude. It is the sign of the failure of subjectivity to justify self-presence as the ground of being.

Power and knowledge are established in a space in which there is no balance of forces. There is no equilibrium in the relations of power and knowledge. The space in which death figures is an asymmetrical space in which the eruption of violence in social relations is the very measure of the imbalance death introduces. Truth cannot be the measured equilibrium of the forces at play between subjectivity and the world. The will to truth cannot be the intention to express that equilibrium. Installed in an asymmetrical space in which experience is made possible by what cannot be experienced, the will to truth must be violence. Knowledge must be power. Power must be objectivity. The scales of truth are only balanced by an act of violence in which the asymmetry of the space of power and knowledge is contorted into the image of a writhing serenity.

Death is the final fracturing of the body, the transgression of the living, visible body in which the body becomes an object of knowledge and the space for the maneuvers of power. *The Birth of the Clinic* describes this transgression. Life is objectified in terms of death and degeneration. And, in *Madness and Civilization*, death is also the power that madness yields. At the end of the fifteenth century, madness replaces the theme of death. *Praise of Folly* replaces Marchant's *Danse Macabre*. Death is not expunged from the world, but installed in the image of madness as, in the nineteenth century, it is in the living body. Death is no longer the limit of existence, but the object of mockery and derision. The substitution of madness for death gives death a tamed form, one in which the futility of existence is made concrete in the everyday experience of the world. "Death's annihilation is no longer anything because it was already everything, because life itself was only futility, vain words, a squabble of cap and bells. The head that will become a skull is already empty. Madness is the *déja-là* of death."[51] This substitution is not a replacement, but a displacement of the same anxiety. The nothingness of existence, the futility of life, is no longer an external threat, but an interior doubt. The domination of the mad in the positivist asylum plays on the erosion of existence prefigured in madness and taking form in subjective guilt. In its ultimate antecedents psychological subjectivity derives from the twisted form—the "torsion within the same anxiety"—in which madness displaced death. The displacement of death into the figure of madness mirrors the contortion of the body in which the body becomes soul.

At every point where power is applied, there is an image of death. The confinement of the mad replaces the exclusion of the leper in *Madness and Civilization*. The plague is the image around which disciplinary power is organized in *Discipline and Punish*. In the application and development of power and knowledge the fear of death is mundanized and interiorized. The effectiveness of the strategies at work in power is not due to the fact that they exorcise death and allay anguish over the futility of life. Rather, these strategies work by their ability to mobilize that fear of death by objectifying death. The effectiveness of power is knowledge. And, the effectiveness of knowledge is the power to delimit objects by drawing around them the lines of nothingness. Power-knowledge makes objects visible by sketching their nothingness.

It is thus not toward nature that Foucault's conception of politics turns, but toward history. The space of the body is not only the space of historical events, but of historical events as the object of politics. Foucault's works must be read politically. Their truth is not their historical accuracy, but their confrontation of contemporary reality with its past. Out of that confrontation comes a new future. "What I am trying to do is provoke an interface between our reality and the knowledge of our past history. If I succeed, this will have real effects in our present history. My hope is my books become true after they have been written—not before."⁵² Foucault's writings, then, are themselves political interventions. They strive to pry apart power-knowledge, to unmask the violence that has wed this couple.

Madness and Civilization, The Birth of the Clinic, The Order of Things, Discipline and Punish, and *The History of Sexuality* are then political works in two senses: they analyze the political complex of power-knowledge, and they are political interventions against power. The first, as we have seen, is the critical work of the historian. The second, a more direct political confrontation, involves the political work, and responsibility, of the intellectual.

Foucault has addressed the problem of the political intellectual in several interviews. Against the totalizing tendencies of power Foucault opposes the dispersed and multiple discourse of theory. Theory is itself a political practice: "Theory does not express, translate, or serve to apply practice: it is practice. But it is local and regional . . . and not totalizing. This is a struggle against power, a struggle aimed at revealing and undermining power where it is most invisible and insidious."[53] In the practice of theory the intellectual rejects the objectifications of power in which he or she becomes power's instrument and object in the domains of knowledge, consciousness, truth, and discourse.[54] The political role of the intellectual is not to represent the working class. Nor is the intellectual necessary for the formation of working-class consciousness, either from the inside, as with Gramsci's organic intellectual, or from the outside, as with Lenin's party intellectual.

Even in his role in the struggle against power in the domain of knowledge, the intellectual is not an exemplar. For Foucault, the bourgeois intellectual is identified with the exercise of language and the advocacy of political conscience. This universal intellectual is a mirror-image of the universal function of the working class in history, with one important difference. The intellectual, because of his relationship as a writer to language, can articulate the truth of history that is lived only unconsciously by the proletariat. The struggle with power and knowledge, however, places other demands on the intellectual. The writer no longer has a "sacral" position vis-à-vis knowledge. Writing is not the primary way in which knowledge is embedded in social relationships. The concrete intellectual is a new type of intellectual who has been politicized within the boundaries of his specific professional activities. Foucault opposes the concrete intellectual to the universal intellectual, thus assuming a shift in the intellectual's place in society. To a universal type, like Zola, Foucault opposes the figure of Oppenheimer, an intellectual whose politics are determined by concrete institutions, and not by the universal values of knowledge, language, and truth.

For the concrete intellectual, political struggle involves the practice of knowledge, where knowledge is specifically linked to power in his professional life. He fights neither against the power of the universal tyranny of repressive force, nor against the lies that hide the universality of truth. For Foucault, the intellectual fights practices in which power establishes techniques and disciplinary codes to regulate knowledge in concrete regions of the social body.[55] Truth is power. It is not merely subjected to power. Thus, the concrete intellectual does not struggle to free truth from the grips of ideology. The politics of the concrete intellectual is a politics of truth, in which the power of truth is turned against the procedures in which truth is produced by capitalist society.

That the concrete intellectual is involved in a struggle over the political anatomy of the body and the political economy of truth is a fact of his historic origins. For it was in biology and physics that this "new, personal style" of the intellectual was created.[56] His antecendents go back, before the appearance of these disciplines, to the professional scholar as distinct from the man of law, the jurist. The significance of the disciplines of biology and physics is that they are formative disciplines for the techniques and strategies in which society gains control over life through the manipulation of death. The politics of the concrete intellectual are a struggle with power, then, in a very specific sense. "The figure of the new intellectual is one who has within his grasp, in league with others, either in the service of the State or against it, powers which can work for the benefit of life or completely destroy it."[57]

History, therefore, is not the only series of events forming in the space of the body. Politics is also a dimension of human existence defined by the political anatomy of the body. Politics and history are both given concrete shape by the struggle for life and death in the fracturing of the individual and the social bodies. Politics is confronted at dispersed points throughout the political body of society with the effects of power-knowledge. These effects are the passage of death over the surface of the body. These are the points at which the body is individualized, atomized, broken into single movements, and turned against itself by a series of techniques that subject it to the power of death. The positivity of power is a function of its ability to fragment, dislocate, and disperse over time. Power is not the repressive force that says no. It is the positive strategy in which the power of the negative, death, is used to gain control over life. Death is not in opposition to life, its contradiction; rather death is in the service of a power controlling life, its extent, duration, and conditions. As in medicine since Bichat, where death individualizes disease in the body, death is part of the positive strategy in which life is administered: "The atomic situation is now at the end point of this process: the power to expose a whole population to death is the underside of the power to guarantee an individual's continued existence."[58] There is a new principle here that has become the strategy of states: to be able to kill in order to be able to live (*pouvoir tuer pour pouvoir vivre*).

What does Foucault oppose to power? Clearly not the barricades. The counterattack is not the construction of another system of power; nor the construction of a political ideology or a political party. In *The History of Sexuality*, Foucault states that the opposition to be mounted against the affective mechanism of sexuality is not to be found in sexual desire, but very simply in bodies and pleasures.[59] Not the repressed sexual body and its secret pleasures, but bodies and pleasures. They are not the same, even if the ruse of the discourse of sexuality has been to convince us that they are identical. The counterattack is thus first of all the weapon of laughter: the laughter of Nietzsche's Overman freed by the death of God. Bodies and pleasures. Not the body and its pleasures, as if there were a natural, phenomenal body which one could liberate from the strategems of the discourse of sexuality. No; bodies and pleasures—plural, hence specific. Their multiplicity and variety must be opposed to the monolithic figure of the sexual body.

But more generally, the counterattack is historical knowledge. Historical knowledge is a transgressive knowledge in which the contortions of the will to truth are unmasked as power-knowledge. To one side Foucault places the history of countinuities, gradual developments, struggles between classes, the evolution of states, and institutions. To the other side is the history of events. In the history of events, there are ruptures and reversals that radically transform the relationship between power and knowledge. History is the history of events producing truth, or the regimes of truth, in Western society. It is also a critique of the ideology, humanism, in which the will is taught to withdraw from the desire for power. Humanism has created a number of "subjected sovereignties," the soul, consciousness, the individual, basic freedom, in which a titular sovereignty was combined with a prohibition upon the desire for power. The critique of humanism exposes two counter-strategies: the "'desubjectification' of the will to power," and "the destruction of the subject as a pseudo-sovereign." The first emphasizes a collective will to power against an individual or representative will. The second stresses communal forms of culture and of social maturation.[60] The answer to power formulated through historical critique is thus a transformed will to power that attempts to break the exercise of power in strategies that implement representative consciousness and political forms of representation.

But this is a strange will to power. It is not force applied to force. It is not the opening of the flood gates of desire against the barriers of repression. It is a will to power formulated in the struggle of history to write, not continuities, but events. It is a political strategy forged in concepts that make it possible to write that dark, brutal history. The counter-attack is against fascism, in which the will is subjected to power by its love for the means used to dominate it. In transgressing the division between truth and lies by exposing power-knowledge in psychology, clinical medicine, and penality, Foucault's writings have opened a discursive space which is also the dispersed, multiplied, and fractured space of the body. The struggle against power occupies that space and uses it to disassemble the totalizing grip of power over life. The will to power that occupies that space, because it is dispersed, is a will to power that is structurally bemused, not fascinated, by the image of power. It is not in love with power.[61]

Foucault's answer to the hegemony of power in Western societies is, thus, not the abdication of power, but the forging of a revolutionary link between power and knowledge. "Revolutionary action . . . is defined as the simultaneous agitation of consciousness and institutions; this implies that we attack the relationships of power through the notions and institutions that function as their instruments, armature, and armor."[62] This revolutionary link disavows the role played by representative consciousness in the concept of totalizing and hierarchized power. "De-subjectified" and "de-individualized," the link between power and knowledge in revolutionary politics, for Foucault, can be summed up in a nomadic joy: a will to wander among bodies and pleasures, before the multiple faces of truth and reason, exulting in an animal madness because it refuses to cut itself off from what it sees and desires.

Discourse, transgression, the body, and death are in the interstices of Foucault's language. They establish the political interpretation of the works required by that language. Foucault is constructing a theory of history and descriptions of historical reversals and transformations which have as their aim a revolutionary will to power.

How should Foucault be read? As politics in which historical events are fixed in a space bounded by the body and by death. History has no meaning, Foucault has said. But there are meanings, in the plural, to be found in history. What a political reading must capture, then, is the singular nature of historical events: ruptures, upheavals, and reversals. What phantoms lurk behind the clear historical events that Foucault's writings have depicted? What are the temptations and possible failures? It seems that Foucault tries to make power-knowledge say everything. But has everything been said about time, the singularity of the event, institutions, critical rationality, and the desires and actions that traverse subjectivity? Foucault has his limit.

4. Problems

LIMITS AND SOCIAL THEORY

How, THEN, is Foucault to be evaluated? Foucault's tactical transgression of normal philosophy, history, and politics makes this a difficult question to answer. Prevailing academic standards do not help us analyze his limits and contributions. Having chosen to work beyond and between the familiar disciplines, Foucault's work is thereby left without a stable identity with respect to which it may be assessed. It is, thus, limited by its own transgressions.

Yet, it would be intellectually indefensible to fail to find some position outside Foucault in order to evaluate him. However, whatever critical stance is taken it must be one that possesses sufficient intellectual proximity that the critique is able to take Foucault seriously. Hence, the dilemma. Foucault's work must be assessed from a point of view which is simultaneously similar yet different. Too similar, and the result is naive praise; too different, and the issues cannot be joined.

We propose, therefore, to evaluate Foucault with respect to the one discursive formation with which he shares a common border, yet of which he is by no means a normally recognizable member: social theory.

SOCIAL THEORY AND FOUCAULT.   Social theory refuses to divorce knowledge from power. It rejects pure theory in its several epiphanies: formalism, whether materialist or idealist;

abstractionism, whether scientific or political; and scientific privilege, whether logical, systematizing, historicist, or hermeneutical. Social theory, thereby, is willing to flirt with ideology and normativeness. It is not, however, anti-science. It rejects the standards of pure science—objectivity, value freedom, formalism, nomothesis—insofar as these are historically lodged in bourgeois social science. But, most generally, social theory, like science, seeks to explain. At its best, however, social theory insists that explanations be just, compassionate, and politically emancipating. Its knowledge, therefore, must account for power: the power of theory to critique existing social orders and to order political practice, no less than objective power in social relations. Social theory opposes pure theory because it opposes domination. As a result, social theorists often live off but not for the institutionalized disciplines which, not incidentally, is roughly what Foucault envisages for the concrete intellectual. Thus, social theory's flaws are a function of its risks. It is social science with a political purpose. Its science occasionally undermines its politics, just as, at other moments, its politics corrupts its science. It is never far from the temptations on either side: pure theory and ideology. It risks these flaws because it clings to the conviction that knowledge and power cannot be separated.[1]

Obviously, Foucault's language is closer to the discourse of modern social theory than to that of the disciplines. One would not readily consider Foucault an academic philosopher, historian, or sociologist. One might read him as a social theorist.

Of course, Foucault does have a relation to the disciplines for those who have need of it. But his history, as we have seen, spills over into politics, as does his philosophy. Therefore, any serious attempt to evaluate Foucault cannot restrict itself to a single perspective or set of theoretical or empirical issues. His concepts, like his relations to the disciplines, are restless, constantly going beyond themselves in search of their opposite. His revolutionary will to power is counterbalanced by an attempt to remake history. This theory of discourse disavows the signifying power of the sign. His historical method is verified by the destruction of its data. His study of rationality relies upon sanity's dialogue with madness. His knowledge discovers truth in an excess, the Unthought. His principal object, the body, is destroyed by the forces that unite it. Social theory as transgression necessarily puts all concepts in question.

Foucault, therefore, is difficult. But clarity is not the basic issue. The critical questions to ask of Foucault are not: Why are you unable to be clear? Why have you not developed and maintained a consistent vocabulary? Why are you unwilling to use others' concepts, or at least to make yours recognizable? Rather, he should be asked: Were the risks of your transgressive method worth the while? Have you gained in explanatory and political force what you lost in parsimony, receivability, and conceptual consistency?

Foucault's gamble, we repeat, is intentional. For Foucault to analyze knowledge in terms of power involves a constant questioning of his own language. If power is in knowledge, then its analysis as knowledge must subject specific concepts to the critique of their own limits. In other words, whatever Foucault gains, at certain points, by his transgressive method cannot excuse him for what he loses elsewhere.

There are, in particular, three questions for which Foucault has not supplied convincing answers. Given the spatialization of time, does time actually remain an active force in Foucault's history? Given the explanatory primacy of discursive formations, is there a subjectivity in Foucault's history? Given Foucault's methodical use of negation, silence, and the unfamiliar, is there ultimately a positive content to his politics? Time, subjectivity, and critical rationality are Foucault's most apparent limits. At each limit Foucault is up against problems in contemporary social theory: the status of the social in social history, the role of subjects in historical action, and the place of rationality in revolutionary politics. Though these problems are widely discussed we present them with reference to contemporary theorists who have most sharply defined or redefined the problems: Braudel and the *Annales* school, Lacan and Kristeva, Habermas and the Frankfurt school—respectively.

TIME. Foucault's conception of history as archaeology does not conform to any paradigm currently at work in history or the social sciences. But it has many points of contact. With the *Annales* historians, Foucault shares an interest in suppressed and neglected topics, a concern for the interdisciplinary context of history, an awareness of the constructive character of historical method, a recognition of the total social fact, and an appreciation of the anonymity of historical structures.[2] With the older positivism of Langlois and Seignebos and more recent *Annales* studies, Foucault's works focus on a history of events. And with the positivist method of van Ranke and traditional history, Foucault concentrates on political history and uses documents for a history of discourse.

But the dissimilarities are just as great. Against the methodology of *Annales*, Foucault rejects the concept of global history, the idea that the subject matter of history is finally society. The anonymity of history is not the stage for the appearance of the works of man. In opposition to positivist history, Foucault attacks the role of psychology as the foundation for the conception of the historical event. Against the concept of linear time and political evolution, Foucault asserts the primacy of rupture and reversal, discontinuity and chance. And, against traditional history, Foucault rejects the idea of political history as a history of statecraft and the intentions at work in diplomacy and war. Nor, for Foucault, is the document the ultimate historical resource. History in Foucault's writings is neither historizing history, nor totalizing history. It is a history that transgresses the epistemological categories of contemporary historiography.

But this transgressive history treads dangerous ground. And Foucault knows it. The theory of discursive formations in *The Archaeology of Knowledge* and the theory of power-knowledge in

Discipline and Punish and *The History of Sexuality* locate the positivity of statements and the positivity of power in fields of dispersion of statements and strategies. The positivity of statements and power does not rest on the prior existence of a plenitude of meaning or of a natural imbalance in the relations between classes. Neither meaning nor social relations as positive categories account for the historical existence of discursive or power relations. Historical existence is a play of differences. The discursive space of statements and the epistemological space of power are negative spaces, dispersions with multiple points of anchorage. They are not concentric circles emanating from an original point.

From von Ranke to Seignebos intentions characterized the singularity of an event in history. Human intentionality gave the event its specific quality as a political maneuver. For Foucault, by contrast, the singularity of an event is the consequence of its irruption in a field with a definite set of relations to other events in the same field. Singularity is the other side of the positivity of the historical event. As a result, Foucault's epistemology spatializes time and overcomes the linear time of historizing, event history. Nevertheless, this is not Braudel's geohistory in which historical exposition involves the dialectic of space and time, the interplay of space and time in the development of institutions, industrial and agricultural techniques, routes of travel, markets, and ideas.[3] For Lucien Febvre[4] and for Fernand Braudel linear time, the homogeneous succession of temporal events, does not explain historical development. In order to explain the rise and fall of markets, the location of cities, and the growth of civilizations, it is necessary to embrace time as a passage of events across the extension of space. Historical time is an extended time, a spatialized temporality.

This dialectic of space and time is absent from Foucault's historical writings. Spatialized time makes it possible to introduce the concepts discursive formation, knowledge (*savoir*), and power. But discursive formations, knowledge, and power do not adhere to locations, to systems of communication, or to cultural networks tied to economic routes and marketplaces. Braudel's *The Mediterrenean*, Bloch's *Feudal Society*, Le Roy Ladurie's *The Peasants of Languedoc*, Georges Lefebvre's *The Great Fear of 1789* have indicated that neither power, nor language, nor knowledge can be separated from geography.[5] There is more, they suggest, to the problematic of power and knowledge than an epistemic strategy. Power and knowledge as exercised in rural and urban societies work in a space crisscrossed by trade routes, valleys and highlands, mountains and rivers.

For Foucault, however, power is an epistemic strategy. Power and knowledge operate in the space of the body, not of geography. This is an important difference and one upon which the significance of Foucault's genealogy depends. But in what terms does Foucault envisage the space of the body? Surely the body in history is part and parcel of those anonymous structures such as land and sea routes, the plan and location of cities, climate and terrain, consumption of meat and grain that have formed the long duration in which events must be conceived?[6] Viewed from the perspective of *Annales* historiography, Foucault's genealogy traces the emergence and descent of power in the fracturing of the body, as part of the space in which the long duration of history unfolds. But Foucault does not clearly situate his own analyses in that context. He has his own good reason. He is not writing a history of the body as one dimension among others, one series of events among others, he is not writing a global history, but a genealogy of power and knowledge in Western societies. His historiographical principle is politics, not total history.[7] But the critical question remains. Are not Foucault's genealogical analyses of power and knowledge limited with respect to the dialectic of space and time in events and in structures of long duration? Genealogy as a historiography contracts the space of time. Beyond the contraction there is a wider and more expansive play of space and time. In short, is the body a sufficient space for a social history of power?

This same question arises with respect to a related but different matter. What exactly is the place of social formations in Foucault's history? To be sure, Foucault is far more clear on this point. There is no geohistory, but there is a history of social relations. However, it is precisely because social relations are prominent in Foucault's analyses that one longs for a more precise theoretical statement of their role. In *Birth of the Clinic* and *Discipline and Punish* the social relations of a nascent capitalist society do act on the body through the clinic and the prison. But here, and especially in *The History of Sexuality* and *Madness and Civilization*, the discursive relations in which the body is fragmented are far more explicitly described than the social relations in which, presumably, that discourse is practiced. The time of social relations is described, often in great detail. In theoretical passages, it is clearly acknowledged. One thinks, for example, of the concept of tertiary, social spatialization in *Birth of the Clinic*, of the concept primary relations in *Archaeology of Knowledge*, and of texts such as the following: "The transformation of a discursive practice is linked to a whole range of usually complex modifications that can occur outside its domain (in the forms of production, in social relationships, in political institutions)."[8] Too frequently, however, the history of discursive relations supersedes the history of social institutions, as in *The History of Sexuality* where the clinic, the family, and the confessional—weakly portrayed—are the only visible social relations. Foucault does not want to reduce history to a history of discourse. This is not semiology. But he exposes himself to these suspicions by his relative silence on social relations. The body has no relation to geohistory. It has a relation to social history. But what, we must ask, is that relationship? Having set out to avoid the traps of class analysis, economism, and traditional theories of the state, Foucault may have left himself with an unintended void. Social relations are visibly present in his histories, but they have no explicit correlate in the invisible, reconstructed space of his history of the body. Is not discourse on the body practiced in social relations? Is not society's time too severely shriveled into the space of discourse?

SUBJECTIVITY.   If the dialectic of space and time is wider than the space of the body in Foucault's genealogy, is it possible that the question of subjectivity is wider than the critique of subjectivity in *The Archaeology of Knowledge* and the historical analyses of *Discipline and Punish* and *The History of Sexuality?* Foucault has discussed the theme of founding subjectivity and its opposite, originating experience, as elisions of the material reality of discourse.[9] Linked to the theme of universal meditation, founding subjectivity and originating experience make discourse the play of signs. Discourse evaporates into the realm of significance. Meaning and significance are merely the correlates of consciousness. Discourse is evacuated of its material density. Exclusions, limitations, and restrictions operate on and within discourse to produce its concrete historical existence. Subjectivity denudes discourse of its positivity.

Foucault's break with subjectivity opens up history. History is at once the history of discontinuities and stable structures.[10] The emergence of discontinuity and stable structures as problems for historical exposition are the result of the transformation of the document into the monument. "In the area where, in the past, history deciphered the traces left by men, it now deploys a mass of elements that have to be grouped, made relevant, placed in relation to one another to form totalities."[11] The consequences of this transformation are the predominance given to discontinuity in history, to general history in opposition to total history, and to a new historical methodology in which the historical fact is the object of a set of strategies that decompose it.

The transformation of the document into the monument also transforms the field of history. The field of history is no longer constituted through the questions put to historical phenomena by the philosophy of history: "the rationality or teleology of historical development," "the relativity of historical knowledge," "the possibility of discovering or constituting a meaning in the inertia of the past and in the unfinished totality of the present."[12] By means of the concepts by which Foucault breaks historical events into levels, series, groups, and regions, he eliminates subjectivity and consciousness as explanatory concepts. It is, in effect, by the methodological and objective rationality of history that Foucault calls into question the idealist assumptions of traditional, historizing history. But, in this move, Foucault exposes his flank. It is frequently asked: Is there no subjectivity in Foucault? What becomes of historical action? And, how can there be historical action without subjectivity? Though seldom acknowledged, Foucault has answers to these criticisms.

The break with subjectivity in Foucault's history is the elimination of the subject as a metatheoretical concept in historical methods. But the founding subject remains as an important object in the field of history. From *Madness and Civilization* through *The Birth of the Clinic* and *The Order of Things* to *Discipline and Punish* and *The History of Sexuality*, Foucault has analyzed subjectivity at work in the formation of modern Western rationality: in the perceptual consciousness and language at the origins of clinical practice, in the formation of the social sciences as philosophical anthropology, in the concept of the soul and idealist subjectivity as the correlates of the imprisoned body, and, finally, in the subjectivity which arises from the self-knowledge objectified in sexuality. In these places subjectivity ceases to be an explanatory concept and becomes an historical problem with which history must contend. His decisive break with idealism, for which the field of objects is grounded in pure subjectivity, requires the creation of a materialist theory of the subject for which the subject is an object to be explained.

What differentiates Foucault's strategy with respect to the subject from the efforts of others, like Jacques Lacan and the *Tel Quel* group, is that the subject becomes a theoretical theme.

As such it is lodged not in a theory of language or discourse, but in a theory of history. For Foucault, the subject is an inscription on the fractured body. Genealogy charts the course of that inscription. For Lacan, language constitutes the subject as the history of desire.[13] The signifier for Lacan is not the representation of consciousness, but is constituted at the line between the signifier and the signified. Here is where the unconscious exists. The signifier, then, is for Lacan the structuring of the unconscious and not the realm of the sovereignty of consciousness or the transcendental subject. The subject as the history of desire comes into being through a rupture in its own continuity (elisions, lapsus linguae, witticisms). The subject is "discontinuity in the real."[14] The division consciousness/unconsciousness is the effect within the subject of desire of the line repression has drawn between the signifier and the signified. The excess of the signifier over the signified, the floating of the signifier in a discontinuous chain of meaning, gives a fundamental primacy to language in the constitution of the subject. The subject speaks from a place (the *id*) where it is not.

For Lacan, the language of the unconscious is always the language of the Other. The Other is the point, external to the subject, in which the speech of the subject is verified and confirmed. Radically decentered and without the possibility of equalizing itself and its unconsciousness, the subject must look to a third witness, the Other, in which to find the juncture of the signifier and the signified.[15] The subject is constituted then in the discourse of the Other, a discourse which reaches into the very structure of the unconscious. There is for Lacan an intersubjective logic imbedded in the role of the signifier in the constitution of the signifying subject. The decentering of the subject, its failure in the face of absolute meaning, extends to its own discontinuity with itself because of the necessity of seeking the confirmation of its own desire and significations in the discourse of the Other.

The role of the signifier in language thus decenters subjectivity. Through language, subjectivity is constituted in its decentering. Language forms the position of the subject vis-à-vis his or her own desire. Lacan, therefore, breaks with the idealist subject, but retains an element of the idealist problematic. The primary significance of meaning still arises through the subject.

Heavily influenced by Lacan's structuralism, Julia Kristeva has turned the Freudian problematic of the symbolic signifier in the direction of a Marxist question of signifying practices. The analysis of the linguistic signifier is for Kristeva, first of all, the analysis of the production of meaning in specific semiotic practices. The concept of praxis, as the productive generation of signification, takes the place of subjectivity. Where Marx only focused on praxis as productive of economic exchange, Freud makes it possible to enlarge the question of the production of meaning. For Kristeva, the production of meaning is not the process in which exchange value is produced, but of the "permutative game which models the production itself." The production of signification in language is thus "the problematic of labor as a particular semiotic system."[16]

Kristeva's concept of the subject, therefore, is not the source of a literary text. It is the process in which meaning is permutated or transformed by a specific practice in which a network of signs is created. Semiotic practices produce texts, not in isolation, but as labor on texts. A literary text, or a segment of discourse, is thus always intertextual. The relationship of the subject to the signifier it uses to communicate its intentions is, thus, the effect of a semiotic practice that has its origins in a social, intersubjective praxis. The subject, in its intentionality, in its positing of objects in the phenomenological sense, is the consequence of a prior positioning of the subject through a semiotic practice. The symbolic is constitutive of subjectivity; subjectivity does not constitute the symbolic. "The subject never *is*, the *subject* is only the *process of signification* and only presents itself as signifying practice, that is when it absents itself *in the position* from which social-historical signifying activity unfolds."[17]

Foucault, too, is interested in the generation of the symbolic, but not as the dialectic of desire or as the subject in signifying practices. Foucault's problematic is the historical production of discursive formations in which epistemic strategies are established. This dialectic of knowledge and power constitutes subjectivity in concrete forms: the asylum, the confessional, and the prison. Subjectivity in isolation and the constitution of the symbolic as a solitary question apart from specific historical configurations are foreign to Foucault. Thus Foucault avoids the problem, basic to Lacan and Kristeva, the problem of the subject as the site of symbolic structures. Relative to Foucault Lacan and Kristeva are not radical departures. Sartre, in *The Critique of Dialectical Reason*, raised the same question in terms of the mediation between social praxis and individual subjectivity. Through what processes or structures, Sartre asked, does individual subjectivity incorporate itself into social formations? The avoidance of this question partly explains the absence of a theory of the subject in Foucault's writings.

There are of course reasons for this absence. First of all, Foucault assumes an ambivalent attitude toward psychoanalysis. If, in *The Order of Things*, psychoanalysis is a critical science which frees desire from subjectivity; then, by contrast, in *Madness and Civilization*, the psychoanalytic theory of the subject conspires to exclude the dialogue of unreason and madness that is essential for the consciousness of rationality.[18] Second, in *The Order of Things* and *Archaeology of Knowledge*, the theory of the subject is understood as philosophical anthropology, a cryptometaphysics. As such it is involved in a long history of metatheoretical substitutions. The subject takes the place and function of the Logos, Being, or God, in classical metaphysics. As a result, one cannot even substitute linguistic structure for the subject without a radical transformation of the metaphysical strategy of centering thought. "I tried to explore scientific discourse not from the point of view of the individuals who are speaking, nor from the point of view of the formal structures of what they are saying, but from the point of view of the rules that come into play in the very existence of such discourse."[19] Third, the disappearance of Man in favor of the contemporary question of language removes the historical necessity for a strong theory of the subject. The subject was an invention of the theory of Man as consciousness. If language replaces consciousness, it does so because Man is no longer the central problem in the human sciences.

These reasons notwithstanding, the problem remains for Foucault. The subject of knowledge is more easily displaced than the subject of desire. It is one thing to dismiss transcendental subjectivity for its complicity in an anthropological epistemology. It is something else to contend with the subject of desire. Perhaps this is why Foucault has turned to the history of sexuality as his latest and major project. Foucault has, it would seem, diagnosed the form of modern self-consciousness in sexuality. Self-consciousness has become the correlate of power, power over life. The objectification of sexuality in the sexual body is the inscription of power on the body. Thus, for Foucault, the history of creation of self-consciousness in the sexual body presupposes the substitution of a theory of the body for a theory of the subject. But even at this point the problem remains. Clearly Foucault does not adopt Merleau-Ponty's solution. The body of desire is not, for him, the phenomenal, lived body. It is not a corporeal, incarnate subjectivity.

Thus, Foucault, like Lacan and Kristeva, rejects transcendental subjectivity. He refuses, however, to turn to semiosis as a solution; yet he, as do they, opens the question of desire. But is it enough to refer desire to sexual self-consciousness, and subjectivity to the body? Desire, for Foucault, is neither expressed in the body, nor is the body the lived form of desire. But can there be desire without a subject? Granting that Foucault admits the subject as an object of historical analysis, does he not, however, leave an unexplained void in the place once held by subjectivity? Kristeva uses desire to create a theory of political action. But Foucault, in limiting desire to the body, does not explain how desire participates in historical action.

One need not reduce historical action to the action of the subject to recognize a problem for which Foucault has no clear solution. His theories of discursive practice and of the concrete intellectual only suggest a solution which is not fully developed. There is more subjectivity in Foucault than a casual reading would suggest. But is there enough to explain historical action, or even to explain the central topics in Foucault's own scheme—events and practices? This question remains even in Foucault's conception of critique and politics.

CRITICAL RATIONALITY. The theory of the subject also involves the question of critical, normative rationality. From the vantage point of a theory of the subject, the Frankfurt critical theorists have raised the question of historical rationality, not from a perspective outside of history, but from within history. They have examined the epistemological conditions for historical knowledge. At the point where Foucault, for the sake of historical method, has eliminated the subject, Adorno inserted a philosophy that would "use the strength of the subject to break through the fallacy of constitutive subjectivity."[20] Similarly, Habermas developed the concept critical rationality from the reason embedded in the interest of emancipation. This is, clearly, the reason of self-reflection at work in the historical formation of subjectivity.[21] For Adorno and Habermas, although they pursue the question differently, the theory of the subject is fundamental to the development of critical rationality and the foundations of historical method.

Like *Discipline and Punish*, Horkheimer and Adorno's *Dialectic of Enlightenment* is concerned with the problem of the constitutive role of power in the formation of subjectivity, society, and knowledge. But there is a difference. In contrast to *Discipline and Punish*, *Dialectic of Enlightenment* is a "primeval history of the subject"[22] that develops the objectivity of social domination in relation to a subjectivity reified by its own search for enlightenment. For Foucault, by contrast, the subject is caught in a field of dispersion and in an exteriority that is irreducible to any internal subjective processes. For Adorno and Horkheimer there can be a history of the subject because the ideas of freedom and self-reflection are by necessity bound together. The concept of freedom to be found in the historical task of enlightenment is the progressive acquisition of the powers of reflection. To reflect on the world is to be guided by an interest in enlightenment. Enlightenment becomes mythic. Hence, the unfreedom to be found in freedom points also to the history of social freedom in terms of the problematic of the subject.

For Adorno, in *Negative Dialectics*, the critique of identitarian thinking—the domination of the concept of identity and logic in thought—is based upon the discovery of the preponderance of the object by means of subjective reflection.[23] Adorno's break with idealist metaphysics, now in the concept of identity, issues from the epistemological conditions for reflection upon the subject. For Habermas, in *Knowledge and Human Interests*, psychoanalysis reveals an interest in emancipation operative in the psychoanalytic dialogue and the effort of the subject to reflect on his own history as a conquest of freedom.[24] Communicative action involves a hermeneutical understanding of life-situations. Language constitutes hermeneutical understanding and involves the ideal equality of the participants in linguistic communication, the ideal speech situation.[25] Habermas, in rejecting the concept of identity, proposes the corresponding possibility of conceptualizing singularity, non-identity, and difference. The universal pragmatics of communicative competence, thereby, point to a rationality which is critical and normative for history and the social sciences.

Normative reason has no such foundation in Foucault's works. Only politics involves a conception of practice with rational norms. But those norms are not explicitly conceptualized and given a critical foundation. It is, nevertheless, possible to argue that in Foucault's analyses of the impact of power upon the body he is beginning to develop a normative theory of politics. His genealogy of the epistemological conditions of historiography and of the conditions of bodily existence presuppose the distortions of the body in history. But Foucault has not elaborated the implications of those conditions, perhaps because he fears the charge of naturalism. Foucault's politics rest primarily on a destructive effort. He seeks to dismantle and decentralize the false unity of power; to struggle against the localization of power in techniques and tactics. However, behind this struggle there is no conception of a social rationality in which politics would become more than an act of negation.

Foucault's politics are not nihilist. But they are clearly antihumanist. For Foucault the question of the normative basis of social rationality in the constitution of subjectivity is inextricably involved with the problematic of philosophical anthropology. When philosophy challenges the sovereignty of the subject in anthropological philosophy and chronological history, it begins to waken from an anthropological sleep. Thereafter thought no longer functions as a transcendental imposition on the empirical fields of life, language, labor.[26] The Nietzschean Return of the Same points to a way out of this dogmatic slumber. It ties the death of man to the death of God and the advent of the Overman. The Return opens up a space in which it is possible to think beyond the confines of anthropologism. "It is no longer possible to think in our day other than in the void left by man's disappearance. For this void does not create a deficiency; it does not constitute a lacuna that must be filled. It is nothing more, and nothing less, than the unfolding of a space in which it is once more possible to think."[27]

The Eternal Return of the Same is not nihilism, but becoming. To will the Return is to will to become again what one was, is, and will be. It is a yea-saying to life, to the will to be: an overcoming of all values viewed in the static light of eternity. In this sense, Foucault's politics is a radical choice for history and for the space of history in opposition to power. Politics is a choice for all the movements of life and thought that have been disfigured in the totalizations of power and knowledge:

neither the asylum, nor the prison, nor the confessional. But then it must be admitted that politics for Foucault is a *via negativa*. Politics is not based upon a positive theory of political practice.

Is a *via negativa* sufficient for politics? Can a critical perspective be introduced into political practice solely through the field made available by a history of dispersed events and radical transformations? Does not a critical theory of history demand an analysis of interests operating in history? Is it possible to speak of a politics of freedom without a theory of the subject as constituted in its historical self-formation through freedom? These are hard questions. And to them Foucault gives only ambiguous answers. He has launched the most ambiguous of projects: a theory of politics and of a political reading of history that claims for itself all the prerogatives of freedom while avoiding the necessity of examining its epistemological and practical conditions.

BEYOND FOUCAULT.   Time, subjectivity, critical rationality form the boundaries of Foucault's archaeology. Each, respectively, is rooted on the near side of the limit, within Foucault's writings: the spatialization of time, the critique of the ideal subject, the politicization of critical history. To the same degree, each, respectively, is in excess of the limit, posing questions Foucault has not answered: Can the body incorporate the social and geohistorical dialectic of time and space? Is desire, apart from subjectivity and, even, language, a sufficient surface for historical action? Without an explicit theory of critical rationality can there be a positive politics? Braudel, Lacan, and Habermas—each, respectively—represent questions to be asked of Foucault.

These fundamental criticisms serve best to limit Foucault and to allow his readers to wonder, with some precision, why read Foucault? Having determined Foucault's limits we are able, with due caution, to consider his contributions, such as they might one day be. From a point outside Foucault, we are free to ask what might he have to say to the issues currently joined in social theory? There are two general questions, which by their sheer persistence and currency must be asked. How is power distributed in society and does this distribution determine the freedom and action of persons? Given the fact that power is historical, hence, in time, maldistributed, how is social explanation possible? The former involves current debates on the state, class, and ideology. The latter involves theory, practice, and historical method.

POWER AND SOCIAL THEORY.   Perhaps it is because the problem is so central that social theory has never been able to negotiate a coherent theory of power. Even though power's relation to knowledge is the raison d'être of social theory, power continues to unleash a series of theoretical obstacles. Is power a negative force imposed on knowledge? How are power relations implicated in class relations? Is power the means of the ruling class? Do the oppressed classes have power and, if not, how is change possible? What is the role of the State in power relations? Is the State merely an instrument of the ruling class, or does it consolidate and apportion class interests? Do power relations determine the content of ideologies and is ideology, thereby, the corrupt opposite of truth? If power dominates the State and ideology as a means of class relations, is there no regulation or governing outside the dominating classes?

These questions are today associated with debates among a number of writers, few of whom would be considered immediate theoretical kin to Foucault: Poulantzas, Miliband, Giddens, Parkin, Gouldner, Offe, Habermas, Althusser, O'Connor, Wallerstein, Skocpol, among others. Foucault, who gives little evidence of having read these others, nonetheless, is quite aware of their questions.

The question of power remains a total engima. Who exercises power? And in what sphere? We now know with reasonable certainty who exploits others, who receives the profits, which people are involved, and we know how these funds are reinvested. But as for power. . . .

We know it is not in the hands of those who govern. But, of course, the idea of the "ruling class" has never received an adequate formulation, and neither have other terms, such as "to dominate," "to rule," "to govern," etc. These notions are far too fluid and require analysis. We should also investigate the limits imposed on the exercise of power—the relays through which it operates and the extent of its influence on the often insignificant aspects of the hierarchy and the forms of control, surveillance, prohibition, and constraint. Everywhere that power exists, it is being exercised. No one, strictly speaking, has an official right to power; and yet it is always exerted in a particular direction, with some people on one side and some on the other. It is often difficult to say who holds power in a precise sense, but it is easy to see who lacks power.[28]

More specifically, almost as though he were a participant in these debates, Foucault has staked out a position. Against the positions which share the assumption that the State is either the central or a relatively antonomous force in power relations, Foucault has explicitly insisted that the State is but one of many power relations. *Discipline and Punish*, for example, is a detailed study of a major agency of the State's control apparatus, the prison. Yet Foucault takes the occasion of this book to develop the theory of power-knowledge, in which power is a general productive force as much as it is a negative repressive action. Power relations are found as much in societal relations of everyday life and knowledge as in the State at the apex of an abstract pyramid of forces.

Discipline and Punish's political economy, like *Birth of the Clinic*'s political anatomy, does not diagram the flow of power through the State apparatus as action on the oppressed. How easy it would have been, for example, to picture the isolated delinquent class as the effect of power working through the police and prison agencies.[29] The temptation is resisted. The delinquent class is segregated; but, more fundamentally, it is pictured as a positive element in the productive relations of society. The State, thus, acts on the individual, but, in the process, a new, general type of individual is produced.[30] The offender, like the indigent patient in *Birth of the Clinic*, becomes a positive object and subject in power-knowledge in bourgeois society. Foucault, clearly, does not deny the negative repressive force of the State. He does, however, insist that power relations are more complex than this. Power has a positive footing even in this incarcerated class upon which even the oppressed poor look with disdain. The State segregates, labels, creates, and oppresses, but it does not thereby exhaust the political economy of power-knowledge.

Against the positions that attempt to demarcate and classify a nomenclature of classes and class factions in bourgeois society, Foucault abandons class as the primary explanatory concept. Class, an organizing concept, remains, but it does not dominate his social theory of power. *The History of Sexuality*, for example, is an extended critique of the traditional repression theory of class power. The differential distribution of sexuality among the aristocratic, bourgeois, and working classes is an essential aspect of his analysis. The power inherent in sexuality does have class effects. "We must say that there is a bourgeois sexuality; and that there are class sexualities."[31] Ironically, Foucault sharpens the concept of class effects in order to show that class explains only partly. The class theory against which *The History of Sexuality* is written holds that the repression of bourgeois sexuality is a function of domination by which working class sexuality is merely the acceptance of an imposed dominant ideology. Instead, argues Foucault, sexuality is a general mechanism. Power has differential effects, and classes do exist, but the power-knowledge of sexuality is not determined unidirectionally by class relations. Power-knowledge is a complex of relations. Its effects are determined differently according to the specific historical formation. Class relations exist. But power-knowledge is the broader, explanatory concept which has as its chief attribute that it can never be abstract. Power is always concrete.

Accordingly, ideology is neither the opposite of truth nor the reflection of an infrastructure. Against the positions embroiled in attempts to define ideology's dependence on or relative autonomy from class relations, Foucault sets aside the science/ideology couple in favor of the problem of truth and power.[32] Hence, *Archaeology of Knowledge*, which is sometimes seen as the foundation for a new, positive science of knowledge in the human sciences, is in fact a radical opening up of knowledge itself.[33] Though power does not figure prominently here as it does later, knowledge (*savoir*) is made ready for the analysis of its complicity in power relations. Foucault employs a double-edged sword. In one direction, knowledge is cut loose from the disciplines and sciences. In the same motion, the science/ideology distinction is severed at the waist.[34] Since knowledge (*savoir*) is not the pure form of science, and science, by the same token, is not the denouement of knowledge, then "ideology is not exclusive of scientificity."[35] Power, class, and the State are not clearly addressed in *Archaeology of Knowledge*, but we do find the structure of Foucault's subsequent theory of power relations. Clearly he must oppose any view that sees ideology as either an instrument of State domination, or as the epiphenomenon of class relations. Knowledge, like power, is specific. Knowledge is in the conflict and struggle of history because it appears, not in ideal form, but in the discursive practices of historical action.

Instead of analyzing this knowledge—which is always possible—in the direction of the episteme that it can give rise to, one would analyse it in the direction of behavior, struggles, conflicts, decisions, and tactics. One would thus reveal a body of political knowledge that is not some kind of secondary theorizing about practice, nor the application of theory. Since it is regularly formed by a discursive practice that is deployed among other practices and is articulated upon them, it is not an expression that more or less adequately "reflects" a number of "objective data" or real practices. It is inscribed, from the outset, in the field of different practices in which it finds its specificity, its functions, and its networks of dependencies.[36]

Ideology, thereby, cannot be segregated from science. This is not an analytic judgment, but a political one. Foucault's concrete intellectual, therefore, is opposed to the universal intellectual. The latter, because he had no specific place in society, transcended even the segregation of science and ideology which went unchallenged. The universal intellectual may have achieved his moral voice by virtue of scientific accomplishments. But that moral voice, with all its ideological intonations, was broadcast apart from science. The universal intellectual used science to maintain a position of moral privilege.[37] By contrast, the concrete intellectual, no less implicated ideologically, speaks through and by means of science. Since science and ideology, to the same extent, are discursive practices, they cannot be considered ideal, moral vocations. They are discursive labors, conditioned by the material forces of their social field. Science and ideology, as knowledge (*savoir*) and knowledge (*connaissance*), are but aspects of general political action. This, quite clearly, is the message of all of Foucault's historical studies. The curious effect of this step is that Foucault here distances himself as much from those who would construct a scientific Marxism as a critical weapon against bourgeois ideology, as from those who cling desperately to the value of freedom of pure science. Knowledge as the politics of specific discursive practices transcends both science and ideology.

State, class, ideology. It would be foolish to claim that Foucault has definitively remarked the field of these concepts. But it would be equally ridiculous to overlook his contributions. Clearly he is aware of the debates. Frankly, we have no idea whether or not Foucault has ever read Habermas, Offe, Miliband, Poulantzas, Gouldner, or the others. And it's not relevant. What is relevant is that, during the period in which Foucault's work has taken shape, others have been preoccupied with the State, class, and ideology; and there are affinities between the two.

During the '6os and '7os the problem of the State received renewed attention once the backs of economistic and humanistic Marxisms were decisively broken. However quaint the early writings of Althusser and Poultanzas may now, in retrospect, seem, they did serve to open the State to critical investigation.[38] Relative autonomy is surely an insufficiently pliable concept to capture the complexity of the State's role in power relations. Nonetheless that very concept did, it seems, drive a theoretical wedge between the State and mode of production. Once it was allowed that the State is even relatively autonomous from economic relations, all the casuistry in the world of last instances could not put the economistic Humpty-Dumpty back together again. Thus, on two sides the State emerged in social theory as a primary social force. With Habermas and Offe,[39] for example, the State is pictured as a governing force bearing historically specific responsibilities in late capitalism. Whatever functionalism or Weberianism colors the German school's idea of legitimation crisis, it does reestablish the theoretical link between the State's control and selection mechanisms and the practical world of norms. In effect, the legitimation crisis is a crisis of the late capitalist State's inherent distance from the practical social democratic values of the controlled civil society. Obviously, there is here an affinity with Foucault's concept of immanent power. Moreover, Foucault's concept power-knowledge at least suggests a specific explanation of the relationship between State control and practical norms, while avoiding the critical theorist's reifications of State action as steering mechanisms and of practical norms as natural residues of a universal telos of freedom.

On the other side, there is growing and more sophisticated political sociology which similarly attacks economic determinism. In this view the State is seen as an autonomous or relatively autonomous force. The claims of economic interests are allowed, but without all the formalism of Althusser and Poulantzas. For example, Skocpol's *States and Social Revolutions*, with its mixture of regard for and criticsm of Wallerstein's world system theory, gains leverage for State action by introducing international politics. Skocpol attempts to dereify the State by insisting that analysis take into account the concrete relations all states must have within the wider world of economic interests and geopolitics. When, in Skocpol's view, states are "understood as potentially autonomous organizations located at the interface of class structures and international situations," political action moves to the "very center of attention."[40]

If Habermas, on the one side, opens the concept of the State to practical everyday rationality, then, on the other, Skocpol opens the State to geopolitics. Foucault, it is clear, is working between these two positions. It is true, of course, that Foucault does not provide an adequate political sociology. His view of the State is too partial, too overwhelmed by the general mechanisms of power-knowledge. But the idea power-knowledge, precisely because it is general, does suggest a sociology of State power that would operate in the theoretical space between the crises of legitimation, on the one hand, and international interests, on the other. Power-knowledge is neither norms nor interests, but more than both. Hence the autonomy Foucault grants to the State, while parallel, is greater than that given by either Habermas or Skocpol. In effect, the State is conceptually freed because it is empirically and not abstractly defined. Foucault's position is limited, of course. Partly because he fails to develop an explicit theory of geohistory and social formations, he defines the State and change too little.[41] But what he does contribute is a general theory of power that corresponds to these attempts to overcome economism, while allowing for the historically concrete relations of the State to practical knowledge on the one hand and international social relations on the other.

Needless to say, discussions in the last two decades on the State were not divorced from those on class and ideology. In fact, the theoretical kinship of these discussions suggests the probable contribution of Foucault to the wider world of social theory. Foucault, we know, followed, if only at a distance, the debates evoked in France by Althusser.[42] We know also, that Althusser, more than any other single writer, had captured the center stage of social theory. The fate of an Althusserian tradition is far from assured. If Althusser's own scheme is in ruins it is because nearly everyone—from social theory's new right through liberalism to the old left—has attacked him at great length.[43] Why so essentially narrow a set of theoretical studies as Althusser's, focusing as they do on technical problems in the reading of Marx, have had this enormous effect, we choose only to guess. Althusser has been the molehill that brought forth a theoretical mountain. These critiques, though different in most respects, converge on at least one point: that Althusser's view of class analysis and its effect on his theoretical method led to abstractions unwarranted by historical fact. This flaw in theoretical method is generally deemed to be at the heart of problems with the Althusserian theories of class and ideology, no less than of the State. Foucault, we would suspect, saw this problem clearly, as did these others.

Poultanzas' attempt to explain while classifying the aspects of class and class factions is the principal case in point.[44] His defense of the empirical content of his analysis does not persuade,[45] although this may be due as much to the difficulty of spelling out the details of a structural explanation, as much as to actual failure to consider empirical materials. In any case, Frank Parkin's bemused summary of the technical problems involved in any attempt to clearly demarcate the levels of class in relation to a theory of causation are compelling,[46] even if his bourgeois argument is not.[47] Debates such as these are of limited interest. What is important in them is the extent to which they have led to a reevaluation of basic concepts. In this regard, the most fertile theoretical discussion to emerge from the attempts to reconsider class analysis has been that on the new class. Obviously, the very idea of the new class presents specific and unavoidable problems which require a reanalysis of class on the one hand and ideology on the other. The very possibility of a new class of managers, or managers and intellectuals, which governs in lieu or on behalf of the ruling class, has reformulated the question of power in social theory. In one direction it has resuscitated the previous generation's concern with the problem of elites.[48] Is the managerial elite an instrument of plural interests or of the ruling class? Or is the new class elite autonomous, or relatively autonomous, from both?

The new class debate has put additional nails in the coffins of the liberal end-of-ideology ideology, no less than of the social democratic pluralist ideology of interests. To take seriously the new class as a class is, simultaneously, to question economistic class analysis and to admit the intellectual elite into the impure realm of managerial ideology. Again, a double-edged sword. In the same movement by which the classes are dissected, the purportedly ideology-free managers are corrupted by association with ideological intellectuals, and vice versa. What, in the end, is Foucault's concrete intellectual, if he is not the same figure of whom the new class theorists, from Touraine through Gouldner, have written?[49] Thus, surely, Foucault has some word to pronounce on both sides of the new class debate. The members of the new class—managers, intellectuals, or both—are not obviously either the owners of the means of production or the sellers of labor power, pure and simple. And, to the same extent, they are neither ideology free nor mindless automatons reflecting external class relations.

In this connection, Foucault's attempts to transcend class analysis, to formulate the politics of the concrete intellectual are worth reading. If, again, Foucault's implicit theory of the new class is subjugated to a general theory of power-knowledge, it does suggest grounds on which class and its effects might be analyzed without reducing everything to class, or nothing to class.

DEATH AND METHOD. But is it really a contribution to raise questions and suggest alternatives at a distance? Yes, only if the position from which the suggestion comes has its own specificity. Foucault's does. What he lacks in the details of political sociology, class analysis, and ideology critique, he has in the contents of a social theory of death, and life. Since Marx's warnings, in 1857, that social analysis must avoid the Robinsonade trap,[50] social theorists have steadfastly avoided questions of life and death. This extreme fear that naturalism would undercut historical method has left a huge silence in social theory. Life and death are unthought in spite of the fact that we have absolutely no doubt whatsoever that political power controls lives and produces death. This is not to say that Marx's warnings are not, even today, pertinent. In fact, contemporary social analysts, like Habermas and Lévi-Strauss, who have ventured to the limit between history and nature have usually fallen into the abyss of naturalism. Lévi-Strauss, his own protests aside, surely falls into a universalism of mental categories from which even his phonology cannot save him. And Habermas, in a remarkably similar way, is not able to describe the a posteriori synthetic aspects of universal linguistic pragmatics with sufficient concreteness to avoid an historicized teleology of the ideal speech situation. For both Lévi-Strauss and Habermas language forms the limit between nature and history. Also for both, language is not specific performance but natural competence.

Foucault succeeds where they have failed because he avoids language as such, *la langue*, in favor of discursive practice. And this, we have shown, is a consequence of seeing discourse at the limit of life and death. Speech for Foucault is neither competence nor performance because it is neither simply knowledge or power. Discourse, rather, is politics practiced against concrete forms of death. Death is concrete because power is tactical knowledge. Foucault has no general philosophy of life and death. There is no naturalism. But he does provide, in great detail, in *Discipline and Punish, Madness and Civilization, Birth of the Clinic, History of Sexuality,* and, even *The Order of Things,* careful descriptions of the play of power as control over life and the production of death. Confinement, morbid anatomy, the analytic of finitude, and sexuality are all articulations of death within theories of life. Critical social theory, for Foucault, is the discourse which transgresses these concrete formations of death. If even social theory participates infinitely in the play of discourse and death, it is only because discourse is historically concrete, not naturalistically universal. The play of historical discourse, therefore, is not a hypothetical infinite regress. Foucault troubles himself not with logical circularity, but with the void. That void is death. Only naturalism tries to provide a positive theory of death. Foucault takes the risk of opening a void because he accepts the political fact that power entails death and, thereby, is a proper and necessary object of social analysis.

Quite obviously this is a consequence of Foucault's methodological tactics. He is aware, as is practically everyone else, of the futility of positivism. But he is not willing to go to the other extreme of theoretical formalism. His solution to the empiricism/rationalism dilemma is surprising and, for this reason, easily overlooked. Obviously, he does not thrust fact and reason back into an abstract dialectic. Nor does he translate them into the theory/practice couple. He uses, of course, the concepts theory and practice, especially in his political essays. And, it is true that his solution to the reason/fact problem is in the relation between theory and practice. But he transgresses even this sacred cow of social theory. Theory does not inform, guide, enlighten, or stipulate practice. And, conversely, practice cannot generate objects for theory. In other words, he would agree with Perry Anderson and others that the crucial lack in contemporary social theory is its loss of attention to political practice, but he disagrees that the answer is to be found simply in Anderson's insistence on a return to a working-class social basis for theory,[51] just as much as he refuses Althusser's formalism of theoretical practice.

For Foucault, theory is practice, and practice is theoretical because knowledge is in power and power in knowledge. There are no dialectics here, except perhaps metaphorically. This is a descriptive statement. Foucault's metatheory is above all political history. As we have seen, this is not simply a moral choice. He is not choosing the concrete over the abstract, the empirical over the theoretical, power relations over epistemology. Instead, he argues, and we think quite persuasively, that, at bottom, there is no choice. One cannot dismiss the meta-physics of rationalism/empiricism with the right hand, and keep essentially the same dichotomy in a left-handed insistence on theory/practice. In other words, Foucault might suggest, social theory has been insufficiently radical and, in this, has failed to reassess everything that must be reassessed. It is necessary to transgress *all*, not just some, of the old dichotomies: theory/practice no less than rationalism/empiricism, supernat-ural/natural, essence/existence. Political and epistemological dichotomies serve merely to draw limits and, in drawing them, they limit the power to transgress. The dichotomies limit the play of thought and action by organizing their contents. Thought and action are against a void, not within a structure or around a center.

Perhaps, therefore, it is to methodology that Foucault makes his most specific contribution. If the epistemological and on-tological dichotomies are rejected, then too must be the dis-tinction between methodology and substance. At its worst methodology assumes a privileged logos prior to fact on the basis of which the concreteness of the world is ordered. Against this purification of science, Foucault criticizes the very idea of methodology. Power-knowledge is the specific field of relations that determines the historian no less than workers, prisoners, patients, or kings. History is leveled. History must describe itself as it describes its world of objects. But this cannot be positivist description. Thus, concrete history's critical function is performed by constantly forcing history to the limit of the visible. History is a reconstruction of the world, to be sure. But its reconstructions do not control the world described. Recon-struction is transgression. History transgresses the limit between fact and knowledge when the visible document, its resource, is read against the descriptions of the regulating forces of history, its topic, by which the document is produced. Thus, as we have shown, this history takes the document as a monument pro-duced by historical action. This transgression, with its risk of falling into a void of unwarranted reconstructions, is itself contested by making history political practice. In effect, politics is the final judge of the truth of history. Viewed traditionally, this is relativism. Viewed from the point of view of Foucault's Nietzschean politics, it is the basic fact. Life, power, knowledge, theory, practice are set necessarily against death—the death of God, the death of man, the death of metaphysics, the death of control. Those who, in the name of science, will their truth by controlling the world of fact are in league with those who willfully control lives by the mystification that life will outrun death. Silence is the basic fact of discourse, including historical and social scientific discourse.

Foucault, thus, joins the current debate on method. Since Marx, social theory has worked in the space between the critique of positivist empiricism and idealizing formalism. In the last decade, social theory and various kindred movements have defined that space with great precision.

In the estuary of the *Annales* movement, Wallerstein has clarified, for social history and sociology, the problem of writing the history of world-systems while trying to avoid the systematizing of systems analysis.[52] Beneath the enticing abstractions of traditional history—the nation-state, the urban center, the imperial power—is a silent history of rivaling modes of production in a world economy, of the countryside, of peripheral states. The kinship of world systems analysis to histories from below—from Bloch and Febvre to Braudel, Hobsbawm, and E. P. Thompson—hardly needs saying.[53] Just as obvious is the requirement that a history of world economies must both transcend and criticize the academic disciplines for their complicity in British-American imperialism.[54] Quite apart from his shared debt to the *Annales* school, Foucault shares Wallerstein's insistence that history must, in large part, be a history of the margins of society for the very reason that traditional history has been the captive discipline of the imperialist core.

In the backwaters of crypto-idealist critical theory, Habermas has enlarged the circle which surrounds pure theory.[55] He has shown that hermeneutics no less than the empirical-analytic sciences controls. If the latter has a technical interest in scientific (hence, political) control, the former is controlled by its inability to diagnose systematic distortions in the tradition it uses to interpret. If Habermas failed to escape a teleology of universal freedom, he did decisively demonstrate, even in this failure, that knowledge cannot be divorced from interests. Though of different provenance, Foucault's political epistemology works in the same region.

In the eddies of American pragmatism, American ethno-methodology has shown that the practice of language cannot be gotten around; that, thereby, formalism in sociology is but a ploy. Garfinkel's ethnomethodological indifference and Ci-courel's claim that all measurement is norm creating work lead to the conclusion that sociological work is practical because practical life is sociological.[56] All social reality is negotiated repairing of contexts. This repair is praxis. If ethnomethodology has virtually nothing to say about social structures, it at least has established the grounds of a critique of scientific privilege. Like Foucault, it has done so with reference to the primacy of discursive practice.

And in the murky waters between structuralist objectivism and phenomenological subjectivism, Bourdieu has developed a theory of practices as the basis for a concrete description of social form.[57] By organizing his work between the concepts *champ* and *habitus*, Bourdieu rids social theory of the objectivist/ subjectivist conundrum and frees sociology to be the empirical description of visible practices informed by socially structured dispositions and performed in social fields of force. In a rough way, Bourdieu's theory of practices contends with the same problems as do the concepts of two very different thinkers: Touraine's historicity and Gidden's structuration.[58] If Bourdieu explains his method too little, and Touraine and Giddens explain theirs too much, they do, nonetheless, share a general concern with Foucault's rejection of the old epistemological dichotomy and his adoption of practices as the topic of social science.

Needless to say, once Wallerstein, Habermas, Garfinkel, and Bourdieu pour into the wider sea of social theory, their arguments are but several of many waves. But if we judge them at the point where fresh water turns to salt, we see a considerable similarity. Each is concerned to move social analysis beyond epistemology, and beyond the academic disciplines. Each turns, though differently, to the practical world peripheral to the great events of traditional social science, and most turn to discourse as a primary form of practice. Each (even ethnomethodology) views social science as the study of concrete political practices. When Foucault is set out in this sea, his social theory floats quite well. In fact, given the variation among these others, Foucault is at least as inventive and specific as any, and perhaps more than all combined.

SILENCE.   The silence of laughter is the key to understanding the violence of transgressive discourse.[59] It is neither the violence of historical relativism which encloses historical events within themselves, nor the violence of the philosophy of history in which events are subjected to the tribunal of the absolute. Historical method, for Foucault, chooses to be its limitations, to live within the contours of its positions, in recognition that it is not the role of historical analysis to remove tensions from the field of events.

Foucault's archaeological discourse, therefore, is the choice of silent laughter over the delusions of the anthropological problematic. Truth is political: a truth that looks for its confirmation in the very actions that its historical analyses engender. Only in the face of an absolute or closed totality is truth without limitations. Within the field of history, to know the limitations of a discourse is to know its positive truth. This positivity does not arise from the negation of the negation; the positive of idealism. It is the positivity that emerges from dispersion, chance, and discontintuity; from the rupture and reversal of events.

Truth, therefore, appears in history in the midst of ruins

brought by the risks it takes. To write history is to wager against the possibility of error. But only to wager. Neither the philosophy of history overshadowed by the absolute nor historical relativism can understand these risks. But Foucault does. And this is simultaneously the strength and weakness of archaeological discourse. Violence is always an unstable action. All the more so is the violent act that transgresses the will to know, that breaks the spell of anthropological sleep, and that digs its own grave by creating a space to think.

Appendix
Concepts Used by Foucault

This glossary does not provide dictionary entries but short presentations of the significance of and problems associated with each concept. It is not intended to stand on its own and should, therefore, be used with the book's index and text, and Foucault's own works. Terms are taken from the standard translations or from our own usages in this book. The French is explained only where a problem exists.

AFFECTIVE MECHANISMS OF SEXUALITY (*disposif de sexualité*). Though translated, in the standard American edition, as "deployment of sexuality," this phrase should indicate a general social mechanism whereby the knowledge and practice of sexuality is dispersed throughout society. The mechanical image should be read to include the basic theme of the active work of power-knowledge in society. The concept appears in *History of Sexuality* and, thus, is specific to the controlling and regulative mechanisms of society on human sexuality. It does not refer, narrowly, to the repression of sexuality. *See also* Power-Knowledge.

ANALYTIC OF FINITUDE. This concept is discussed at length in *The Order of Things* (pp. 312–18). For Foucault, the finitude of Man and the finitude of knowledge involve each other and both are social conventions formed in the nineteenth century. This century gave birth to liberal modernism and specifically the human sciences. The birth of the human sciences is coterminus with the anthropological idea that Man is the center of history but this history is one that conditions and limits Man. Thus, the political economists and even Marx (at least the young Marx) described value as the product of labor over against the alienating forces of capitalism (Marx) and the threat of death through overpopulation (Malthus). No less, human knowledge was understood as finite, unable to achieve pure reason, and thus required to think from a point within consciousness (Kant). The analytic of finitude, therefore, is a philosophical anthropology in which Man's finitude opens up his subjective consciousness, which in turn is the source of truth. The human sciences, as a result, are those sciences which were built on the idea of Man's finitude and therefrom constructed the possibility of making Man both the object and the subject of knowledge. Foucault here joins Heidegger, Nietzsche, Derrida, and others in assuming that the analytic of finitude, even in its rejection of metaphysics, remains a cryptometaphysics. Man simply replaces God, Power, Truth, Being, Logos as the center of thought. *See also* Anthropological Sleep; Anthropology; Man.

ANTHROPOLOGICAL SLEEP. An expression used explicitly in *The Order of Things* (pp. 340–43), anthropological sleep refers to the effect of philosophical anthropology on social thought. Foucault holds, following Nietzsche, that anthropology, or anthropologism, dulls mind and morals to the disruptive effects of power and death on human life. Man is understood as a controlling center wherefrom a falsely held will to truth creates the illusion of pure truth behind which power secretly operates. *See also* Anthropology; Man.

ANTHROPOLOGISM. *See* Anthropological Sleep; Anthropology; Man.

ANTHROPOLOGY. This term does not refer to the specific science of man, but to an ideology-laden philosophic point of view; literally, a logic of man. Anthropologism is, for Foucault, the philosophical foundation of all human sciences which were born in the nineteenth century. In a word, it is an ideology which privileges Man as the center and source of the philosophical and human sciences. As such, its influence extends well beyond the human sciences. *See also* Anthropological Sleep; Man.

BODY. The body is Foucault's principal empirical object of investigation. His histories of bodies (in hospitals, clinics, prisons, and elsewhere) are less the consequence of a general philosophical interest than of an historical and political judgment. Foucault claims that the birth of the liberal age was coterminus with the development of strategies for controlling for political purposes the bodies of potential workers. However, the body is also a general problem insofar as it is the site of death which is the ultimate limit on knowledge. However, it should be understood that Foucault is primarily interested in the body as an empirical topic to which this general theory of bodies, death, and limits is juxtaposed. *See also* Limit; the Other.

DEATH: *See* Limit.

DISCIPLINE(S). Foucault's historical studies are, essentially, studies of the birth of the modern social scientific disciplines, in particular: psychiatry and psychology, clinical medicine, the human sciences, penology, political economy, and the various pedagogical and clinical practices aimed at controlling sexuality. These disciplines are, thereby, understood as means for disciplining human powers for the economic needs of modern industrial society. The double entendre, thereby, expresses Foucault's most Marxian idea: that the social scientific disciplines were crucial to the capitalist mode of production's requirement that labor power be disciplined as the basic means for controlling productivity, hence increasing surplus value necessary for the accumulation of capital. *See also* Knowledge; Will to Truth.

DISCONTINUITY. This term, clearly akin to the Bachelardian and Althusserian notion of rupture (*coupure*), is one of the tags with which readers of Foucault often oversimplify his method. It is, therefore, a point of controversy and difficulty in reading Foucault. On the one hand, it is clearly the case that Foucault sees history as marked by discontinuous moments. On the other, in his historical studies, he obviously holds that even radical transformations take place over time. In the former connection, he opposes linear theories of history, which hold that the new evolves continuously out of the old. But, in the latter regard, he does not believe that the new occurs all of a sudden with no relation to the old. Change in history is, rather, radical transformation of the relations among the parts of society, not *creatio ex nihilo*. As with many of Foucault's basic concepts, it is necessary to search patiently for the nuances Foucault introduces as his discussions proceed. Also, it is best to check the abstract concept against his actual empirical studies wherein those nuances take shape. *See also* Episteme.

DISCOURSE. Roughly put, discourse is simply language practiced. In the lexicon of modern linguistics, discourse is distinguished from the formal aspects of language (Saussure's *la langue*) and the specifics of actual speaking (*la parole*). Discourse is understood to have its own rules of operation and, empirically, to have its own forms. However, as a more inclusive instance of language use, its analysis is limited neither to the customary elements of linguistics (semantics and grammar) nor to linguistic's basic units (the sentence, the proposition, or the speech act). Discourse, therefore, is susceptible to analysis in relation to the other aspects of social life: politics, culture, economics, social institutions. Generally speaking, Foucault adds no unusual meanings to the term, even though, in his method, it is the means by which he focuses attention on the analysis of specific social practices, namely discursive practices. Discourse is obviously central to Foucault, but it is also a troublesome topic in that he seems to relate discursive practices to social practices but without ever providing an explicit answer to the question, where does discourse end and social life as such begin, if at all? *See also* Discursive Formation.

DISCURSIVE FORMATION. This concept is discussed most explicitly in *Archaeology of Knowledge* (part 2). It is, generally, Foucault's means for acknowledging the fact that discourse is an empirical phenomenon situated in a field of complex social forces and their relations. The best-known, but also troubling, use of the concept is the term episteme in *The Order of Things*. An episteme is a set of social conditions which require and permit particular historical forms of discourse and knowledge in the Renaissance, the Age of Reason, and the nineteenth and twentieth centuries. As with his general theory of discourse, it is often difficult to determine the precise distinction between a discursive formation and a social formation, in the Marxian sense. *See also* Discourse.

DISCURSIVE PRACTICES. *See* Discourse; Discursive Formation.

DISPERSION. This term appears frequently in Foucault's theoretical texts, but no consistent effort is made to give it a technical definition. Its frequency of appearance reflects Foucault's attack on metaphysical discourses which center thought around axioms, principles, origins, essences, or meanings. If centered thought is controlled, then dispersed thought is relational and relatively free, though not relativized. Dispersion characterizes Foucault's fundamental methodological premise that the events studied by the historian should be understood as arranged in discrete series, each of which has its unique time. In *Birth of the Clinic*, for example, the medical, political, economic, and epistemological series of events are pictured separately dispersed throughout a relational space. This allows Foucault to describe the rise of clinical medicine in relation to the separate births of the modern state, the new industrial society, and the modern social scientific disciplines. Underlying the term dispersion is, of course, a spatial image by which Foucault's critique of historicism is revealed no less than his affinity for the Annalist notion that long-enduring times are spatialized.

DOCUMENT. The problem of the document in history is to preserve its materiality while acknowledging that documents never contain the full truth of history. Foucault wishes to avoid the hermeneutic practice of treating documents as mere windows through which deeper meanings are to be interpreted. On the other hand, the document is the basis upon which the contents of history are reconstructed. This involves a positive theory of the historian's document in which documents (court records, census tabulations, letters, stories, shipping manifests, clinical notes, and so forth) are understood as discursive practices conditioned by the same regulative mechanisms that determine social practices as such. As a result, by analyzing a document's rules of formation, one reads the social practices of the time under study *in* the document, not *through* the document. The document is a positive, material entity itself and this is why Foucault, in *Archaeology of Knowledge* (pp. 138–40), prefers to substitute for it the term *monument*.

EPISTEME. This term is used most specifically in *The Order of Things*, a study of the historical periods surrounding Foucault's anthropological century, the nineteenth. The Renaissance, the Age of Reason, the Modern Age, and post-Modernity (roughly the twentieth century after Freud) are viewed as discrete social and discursive formations, each possessing similarly discrete social and discursive practices. Foucault admits that in *The Order of Things* he employed the term in a somewhat too formal manner, such that the book was open to the charge of being structuralist. Thus, in this book, it appears as though the four epistemes are separated by unbridgeable discontinuous breaks, with the further consequence that the separate formations are too readily interpreted as being obedient to abstract, formal rules and lacking in historical concreteness. The prudent reader will use the term *episteme* cautiously, if at all. One can understand Foucault very well without it. *See also* Discontinuity.

EPISTEMOLOGICAL PROFILE. A term used by Gaston Bachelard to account for the fact that scientific theories always contain philosophical residues. Its broader implication is that science is never entirely free of ideology and that the history of science should not insist on such purity. Though Foucault does not use this term, the concept lies behind the conviction he shares with Bachelard that the history of science must be as much the history of error as of truth. If science always contains philosophical residues, then scientific propositions are not pure truth. They contain the errors of the scientist's inability to purify his thought of ideas which come from previous errors in science, outmoded theories, and philosophical tensions typical of all rational thinking. In Foucault, the history of errors is also related to his very Nietzschean critique of the will to truth, in science, as in politics. *See also* Will to Truth.

EVENTS. At once an important and easily misunderstood concept, events are the basic units of Foucault's historical method. Foucault keeps his distance from *histoire événementielle*, or the history of great events. Foucault, like the Annalists, refuses to restrict history to the study of the grand moments in history: treaties, wars, kings, and the like. Events is a leveling concept. Events are specific. They are moments of reversal in discourse, thought, and practice. As such, they are no more likely to be the domain property of the great than of the ordinary in history. Furthermore, events are specific points of conflict in respect to which social practices are transformed.

EXTERIORITY. *See* the Other.

HISTORY. As with most of Foucault's enterprises, his idea of history is largely defined with reference to what it is not. He does histories of knowledges (*connaissances*), while rejecting traditional intellectual history. He believes that history itself is an arena of conflict, but he refuses to label his perspective simply Marxian (though he does seem ready to accept the label Nietzschean). He holds that history is interrupted by major transformations in the relations of society, but he could not be called Althusserian. He holds that even the important transformations in society involve the conjuncture of ongoing series of events, but he is a stern critic of linear and historicist history. Perhaps the most distinctive feature of Foucault's view of history is that, as a type of knowledge, it must allow for reversal, discontinuity, and conflict because, as a real world process, it is intensely political. If history is an arena of struggle, then the study of history must take its cues from specific events in which power and knowledge enforce each other in the practices of social actors. As a result, Foucault's theory of history must be understood in relation to his politics and his philosophy, and history itself can be reduced neither to ideas nor class relations, neither to knowledge nor power.

KNOWLEDGE. Foucault benefits from the two senses of the word in French. He uses *connaissance* to refer to the formal knowledge of an established discipline. *Savoir*, by contrast, refers to knowledge in general, knowledge dispersed concretely throughout a specific historical social formation. For example, clinical medicine, which developed a specific set of rules, is *connaissance*; while the variety of political, economic, medical, and practical knowledges, in their mutual relationships to each other in the early nineteenth century, is *savoir*. Though *savoir* includes practical, everyday life knowledge, it is a much broader concept. `Savoir* could be described as the totality of knowledges (including but not limited to *connaissances*) were it not for the danger of implying something abstract and totalizing. *Savoir*, for Foucault, is distinctively specific, as is best indicated by the fact that he came to associate it with the concrete tactics of power in society. Foucault employs this double meaning in at least two crucial places. First, it is important to the notion of discipline as both disciplines (*connaissances*) and the general tactic of disciplining (*pouvoir-savoir*) the bodies of persons. Second, his own method turns on the assumption that the discipline history (a *connaissance*) must work in constant recognition of its own embeddedness in the *savoir* of its time and of the time it seeks to reconstruct. *See also* Discipline; Document; Power-Knowledge.

LANGUAGE. *See* Discourse.

LIMIT. A concept to be understood in relation to Foucault's idea of transgression, limit represents the basic problem that must be solved when one acknowledges that power is ultimately related to power. If knowledge participates in power's attempt to control men and life, then similarly knowledge is involved in the setting and enforcement of limits on thought and social action. Foucault's critique of the analytic of finitude (in *The Order of Things*) challenges the liberal, modernist attempt to incorporate limits within a theory of knowledge. Humanist cryptometaphysics, no less than classical metaphysics, imposes the limit of the Center. If the former does so deceptively, under the comforting guise of its humanism, it controls no less. Seeking an alternative to these deceptions, Foucault (relying on Nietzsche and Bataille, among others) associates the idea of limit with the sociological concept taboo. Limits, no more than taboos, cannot be destroyed, but they can be transgressed. Thus, for Foucault, history is a critical practice insofar as it conceives of its truth as the product of a constant transgression of the limits on knowledge. Or, in other language, history is a critical investigation of political strategies for concealing the truth of the distortions of power in social life. History thus defined does not believe in an ideal truth, free of these distortions. Limits are given and effectively natural to knowledge, but this does not mean that they cannot be exposed, even if in exposing them they are reinforced. An exposé of the repressive effects of liberal prison reforms will serve equally the managers as the critics of such a system. *See also* the Other.

MAN. Man should be understood as a historically concrete aspect of the liberal episteme. As such, Man is an aspect of *savoir* on the basis of which particular *connaissances* arose in the nineteenth century. Man, the conceptual object of the human sciences, becomes visible as an object because of the specific relations of power-knowledge in the nineteenth century. Man, for Foucault, is a general figure for characterizing the liberal humanism within which Man, the object, thrives. *See also* Anthropological Sleep; Anthropology.

THE OTHER. This ambiguous concept is used by Foucault to characterize the problem of the subject. If one attempts, as does Foucault, to criticize the anthropological notion that knowledge is rooted in the subjective consciousness which in turn is taken as a medium for an original truth, then knowledge must be relational. Thinking must be understood as a relationship to an exteriority. Foucault's solution, however, is not that of phenomenology, and kindred movements, in which the Other is the Alter of a subjective Ego and, as such, a mere displacement of subjectivity into intersubjectivity. Foucault's Other is the Unthought, a theoretical space, itself without limits, which defines the limit of socially acceptable thought. Death, therefore, plays an important role in Foucault's scheme because death figures in the same space of limits in which thought operates. Thought is not the expression of the inner truth of the Subject, but a practice in a complex set of relations. In Foucault's writings, therefore, everything is stated with respect to that which it is not, hence in a void that cannot be formally described. This is why Foucault's writings always situate his concepts and descriptions in unfamiliar terms. He constantly attempts to push his thinking beyond what he and others know. This, of course, is the most explicit intrusion of Hegel into Foucault's thinking, though his relationship with Hegelianism is even more ambivalent than that to Marxism. *See also* Limit; Transgression; the Unthought.

POSITIVITY. Foucault is sometimes accused of being a positivist and, on one occasion, he admitted to being willing to live with the label if critics could think of nothing better. The charge owes to the naive assumption that he is founding a structuralist history, which is an illusion derived from his stern rejection of hermeneutic methods. Foucault opposes any historical method which assumes that the truth of history is a secret meaning uncovered behind documents through their interpretation. In contrast to hermeneutic methods, Foucault wants to establish the positivity of documents, and through them, the events he analyzes. But there is absolutely nothing in Foucault's writings to warrant the assumption that he uses formal axioms and rules (structuralist or otherwise) to deduce empirical facts. He does not believe in an empirical world of free-standing phenomena awaiting the scientist's measures to become facts. Rather, his historical method emphasizes the reconstruction of the positivity of rules operating in history on concrete social practices. Since rules, in his sense, are not givens, they must be reconstructed by the historian. He here contends with the age-old problem of structural method. Social rules and other social mechanisms of regulation are not observable. But they must be reconstructed. Foucault wants reconstruction to be based on the descriptive materials available in documents, not on abstract formal codes or unwarranted interpretations. The positivities in Foucault's histories are the described social formations giving rise to clinical medicine, the modern prison, sexuality, and so forth.

PRACTICES. Practices are the means of historical action. They are, therefore, the empirical objects of historical research to be examined with respect to the regulatory mechanisms of society. Practices are neither the expression of an individual's intentions nor forms dictated by social structures. Foucault attempts to avoid the old objectivism-subjectivism dilemma by studying practices which are both structural and subjective, yet neither simply. He believes that history is a series of events, struggles, and conflicts within which power and knowledge are simultaneously diffused. For example, the practice of incarceration in the modern prison is enacted by concrete individuals but made possible, even necessary, by a general knowledge (*savoir*) of Man and specific theories (*connaissances*) of penality. Thus, the controlling power of incarceration is a practice which is powerful because it is also general knowledge. Practices are, therefore, always tactical, the application of knowledge for a political purpose. Accordingly, Foucault's idea of the historian's practice is subsumed under a general theory of practices. The concept should not, however, be read merely as the practice in social theory's famous doublet, theory/practice. Foucault does not offer an explicit theory of practices except obliquely in *The Archaeology of Knowledge*'s discussion of discursive practices. *See also* Discourse; Discursive Formation; Power-Knowledge.

POWER. *See* Power-Knowledge.

POWER-KNOWLEDGE (*Pouvoir-savoir*). This concept appeared clearly with and after *Discipline and Punish*, though it is present implicitly throughout. Its most important consequences are the following: Power-knowledge assumes that power is not from the top down, from a dominant class upon a dominated class; power is immanent, diffused throughout society, on all levels. Second, knowledge (*savoir*) is not ideal and abstract, but material and concrete; it cannot be divorced from the workings of power throughout society, again at all levels. Third, as a consequence of the second, science cannot be arbitrarily divorced from ideology because science, as a form of knowledge (*connaissance*), is embedded in power relations (*pouvoir-savoir*). Readers would do well when they encounter in Foucault instances either of knowledge (*savoir* or *connaissance*) or of power and control to ask: Where is the effect of power in this knowledge, or the displacement of knowledge in this power tactic?

SUBJECT. Foucault understands the Subject to be one of a series of historical substitutions for the idea of a center which controls thought. It should therefore be placed alongside traditional metaphysical principles: God, Logos, Ousia, Reason, Being, and so forth. The Subject, however, is the central principle of the Modern Age, the nineteenth century. As such, it is a principle essential to the concept Man. In particular, Foucault's critique of the Subject is a critique of phenomenology and other subjectivist philosophies that dominated French thought in the post-World War II period. He shares the widely held and obvious view that modern subjectivisms are the extension of the Kantian notion of transcendental Subjectivity with which, in part, nineteenth century reasoning began. *See also* Analytic of Finitude; Anthropological Sleep; Anthropology; Man.

TRANSGRESSION. This concept is fundamental to Foucault's idea that power and knowledge cannot be divorced. If knowledge is implicated in power, then it follows that there can be no pure knowledge. Foucault's critique of anthropological thought is part of his critique of all traditional forms of thinking in which it is held that knowledge, or truth, can be a pure achievement apart from the conflicts of history. Traditional thought, therefore, relies on purifying technical devices: the syllogism, deduction, induction, and interpretation, all of which assume it is possible to uncover the essential principles of the truth. If, on the other hand, one rejects these epistemological strategies (as one must if truth is related to power), then they are seen as attempts to control both thought and action. As an alternative, Foucault holds that knowledge is gained only by the criticism of knowledge. Thinking, therefore, is a continual transgression of established norms of truth. Thinking is a political act because these norms are socially constructed and maintained. See also Limit; the Other; Power-Knowledge; the Unthought; Will to Truth.

THE UNTHOUGHT. The Unthought relies on the assumption that knowledge, being historical, not pure, is always created by the imposition of some limit. Knowledge is controlled knowledge. Beyond its limits is knowledge, which, in a given historical period, is forbidden or otherwise ignored. Beyond the incest taboo, for example, is always the very idea of incest, a social unthinkable. The Unthought, therefore, forms the limit within which actual knowledge is produced. The Unthought involves the concept of the Other. Thinking is Man's reflection on the Other in which he knows himself. It can also be considered as politically suppressed knowledge that must be exposed. Therefore it is one of those elements of nineteenth-century thinking that entail a critique of its own anthropologism. Foucault's discussion of the Unthought in *The Order of Things* (pp. 322–28) is one of the points at which it is clear that discontinuity does not, for him, imply an unbridgeable chasm between periods. The Unthought is both a necessity for nineteenth-century liberalism and the seed of its ruin. *See also* Limit; the Other; Power-Knowledge; Will to Truth.

WILL TO KNOWLEDGE. *See* Will to Truth.

WILL TO TRUTH. The will to truth is used interchangeably with the will to know (*la volonté de savoir*) or the will to knowledge when knowledge is understood as the pure knowledge Foucault criticizes. This is Foucault's most explicitly Nietzschean idea. Actual knowledge in society is a political activity which attempts to mask the role of power in knowledge. The ideal of the will to truth, hence, is a norm by which power seeks to protect itself by mystifying its control over knowledge. The critique of anthropological thought, therefore, is the most prominent of Foucault's deconstructions of social forms of knowledge. Behind the gentle mask of Man in the human sciences Foucault uncovers political tactics aimed at controlling persons in mental hospitals, hospitals, prisons, bedrooms, confessionals, classrooms, and psychological counselors' offices. In all these places the manifest activity is an attempt to instill, develop, or rehabilitate the truth of Man in men. In fact, they are the use of knowledge to control men's unreason, physical frailty, and moral defects to the end of producing a disciplined population of workers. *See also* Discipline; Limit; the Other; the Unthought.

Notes

In addition to the chapter notes, please see the chronological list of Foucault's Publications, which provides additional bibliographic information. Lowercase letter notations added to the year of publication in the chapter notes refer to entries in this list. Readers may use this cross-reference to seek the most readily available or desired source, whether French or translation (if available). Notes refer always to the source mentioned in the note. Occasionally the French is cited even when a translation exists.

We have quoted where possible from translations of Foucault's works. We changed translations (or referred to the original French) only where necessary. The only major problem in this practice is with *Madness and Civilization*, which is a translation of the abridged edition of *Folie et déraison: Histoire de la folie à l'âge classique*. In this case we cite the latter when referring to materials not in the shortened version and, otherwise, use the American version. The places where we differ from the translations, or considered it prudent to refer readers to the originals, are clearly indicated in the text or notes.

1. Foucault's Field

1. Foucault, *The Order of Things: An Archaeology of the Human Sciences* (*1966a*). pp. xxi and xxiv.

2. See also Foucault's semiological study of Magritte's painting, *Ceci n'est pas une pipe* (1973a); and his presentations of J. P. Brisset's *La Logique grammaire* (1970f) and Arnauld and Lancelot's *Grammaire générale et raisonée* (1969b).

3. Foucault, "Truth and Power," (*1977a*). Other discussions of his politics are: "On Attica" (*1974a*); "Power and Sex" (*1977g*); and various essays and interviews collected in translation: Donald Bouchard, ed., *Language, Counter-Memory, Practice* (*LCMP*) (Ithaca, N.Y.: Cornell University Press, 1977), part III; Colin Gordon, ed., *Power/Knowledge* (*P/K*); (New York: Random House, 1980); Meaghan Morris and Paul Patton, eds., *Michel Foucault: Power, Truth, Strategy* (*PTS*) (Sydney: Feral Publications, 1979).

4. In *LCMP*, see: on Blanchot, "Language to Infinity" (*1963g*); on Flaubert,

"Fantasia of the Library" (*1967c*). And elsewhere, see: on Mallarmé, "Le Mallarmé de J. P. Richard" (1964c); on Roussel, "La Metaphorphosé et le labyrinthe" (1963e), and *Raymond Roussel* (1963a). Also see: "La Prose d'Actéon" (1964a); "La Pensée du dehors" (1966b). And see Foucault's presentation of, among others, Georges Bataille, *Oeuvres* (1970e).

5. For general discussions of the effect of Paris on French intellectuals see: Charles Lemert, "Reading French Sociology," in Charles Lemert, ed., *French Sociology* (New York: Columbia University Press, 1981); Sherry Turkle, *Psychoanalytic Politics* (New York: Basic Books, 1978); Raymond Boudon, "The Freudian-Marxian-Structuralist (FMS) Movement in France: Variations on a Theme by Sherry Turkle," *Journal of the Tocqueville Society* (Winter 1980), 2(1):5-24; Terry Clark, *Prophets and Patrons* (Cambridge: Harvard University Press, 1973); Diana O. Pinto, "Sociology as a Cultural Phenomenon in France and Italy: 1950–1972," Ph.D. dissertation, Harvard University, 1977; Pierre Bourdieu and Jean-Claude Passeron, "Sociology and Philosophy in France since 1945," *Social Research* (Spring 1967), 34(1): 167–212; and Regis Debray, *Teachers, Writers, Celebrities* (London: New Left Books, 1981).

6. Foucault's writings are a foremost example, namely: *The Archaeology of Knowledge* (*1969a*).

7. Actually Foucault's first book was *Maladie mentale et personalité* (Paris: Presses Universitaires de France, 1954), which was revised and retitled in 1962, then translated as *Mental Illness and Psychology* (New York: Harper & Row, 1976). *Folie et déraison: Histoire de la folie à l'âge classique* (1961a) was his first major book. *Madness and Civilization* is the 1965 translation of a 1962 abridged edition to which Foucault added sections from the French original. A second French edition, 1962, includes two important essays, one of which is Foucault's response to Derrida: "My Body, This Paper, This Fire" (*1972d*). Alan Sheridan offers an explanation for and description of the histories of these texts in *Michel Foucault: The Will to Truth* (New York: Methuen, 1980), pp. 1–8.

8. See, respectively, Foucault's discussions of ignoble events in: "Prison Talk" (*1975c*); *The History of Sexuality*, vol. 1 (*1976a*); "Preface," *Herculine Barbin* (*1980d*); *I, Pierre Rivière, Having Slaughtered My Mother, My Sister, and My Brother . . .* (*1973b*); *Ceci n'est pas une pipe* (1973a).

9. Foucault, *Discourse on Language* (*1971a*), in *Archaeology of Knowledge* (*1969a*), p. 231.

10. Foucault, *Archaeology of Knowledge* (1969a), p. 229.

11. Claude Lévi-Strauss, *Tristes tropiques* (1955; New York: Atheneum, 1974); Louis Althusser, *For Marx* (1965; New York: Vintage Books, 1970); A. J. Greimas, *Sémantique structurale: Recherche et méthode* (Paris: Librairie Larousse, 1966); Nicos Poulantzas, *Political Power and Social Classes* (1968; London: New Left Books, 1975).

12. Foucault, *Archaeology of Knowledge*, p. 15.

13. Jacques Derrida, *Speech and Phenomena* (1968; Evanston, Ill.: Northwestern University Press, 1973), *Writing and Difference* (1968; Chicago: Uni-

versity of Chicago Press, 1978), *Of Grammatology* (1968; Baltimore: Johns Hopkins University Press, 1974); Gilles Deleuze and Felix Guattari, *Anti-Oedipus: Capitalism and Schizophrenia* (1972; New York: Viking Press, 1977); Pierre Bourdieu, *Outline of a Theory of Practice* (1972; Cambridge: Cambridge University Press, 1977).

14. See Turkle, *Psychoanalytic Politics.*

15. For a discussion of these events with respect to changes in sociology, see Lemert, *French Sociology*, essay 1.

16. Foucault, *Discourse on Language* (*1971a*), pp. 232–33. On the related change in his view of power, see "The History of Sexuality" (*1977f*), *P/K*, pp. 201–8; and "Two Lectures" (*1976f*), *P/K*, pp. 78–89 and 93.

17. Foucault, *The History of Sexuality* (*1976a*), pp. 92–102. Hereafter the title *The History of Sexuality* refers to volume 1 of the multivolume work.

18. Foucault, "Truth and Power" (*1977a*), pp. 301–7. On the theoretical status of the individual as subject of power and historical transformation, see "The Confession of the Flesh" (*1977i*), *P/K*, p. 230.

19. Foucault, *Mental Illness and Psychology*, (*1954a*), pp. 86–88.

20. Foucault, "Sur les façons d'écrire histoire" (1967d).

21. Foucault, "Power and Sex" (*1977g*), p. 153.

22. Foucault, *Discipline and Punish: The Birth of the Prison* (*1975a*), p. 221; compare pp. 218–24.

23. Foucault, *Madness and Civilization* (*1961a*), p. 229.

24. Foucault, *Birth of the Clinic* (*1963b*), p. 85.

25. Foucault, *History of Sexuality* (*1976a*), p. 141.

26. Foucault, "Prison Talk" (*1975c*), p. 15. Extract is authors' translation of 1975c.

27. *Ibid.*, p. 15; and "Truth and Power" (*1977a*), pp. 294–95.

28. Foucault, *History of Sexuality* (*1976a*), p. 94.

29. Foucault, "Truth and Power" (*1977d*), p. 298.

30. For Foucault's discussions of the Unthought see especially *Order of Things* (*1966a*), pp. 322–28, and *LCMP*, part 1. The Unthought is one of several concepts Foucault uses both as a resource and an object of criticism, see entry in the appendix, Concepts Used by Foucault.

31. Fernand Braudel, *The Mediterranean* (2 vols.; New York: Harper & Row, 1972), pp. 11–24; Althusser, *For Marx, passim*, but especially p. 257. It should be understood that here, and elsewhere, we are not talking about direct personal influences on Foucault. Foucault himself pays tribute to three teachers—Jean Hippolyte, Georges Dumézil, and Georges Canguilhem (see *Discourse on Language* (*1971a*), pp. 235–37). In the present connection, Dumézil and Canguilhem, are, of course, the teachers who biographically link him to the *Annales* and Bachelardian traditions, respectively. But here we refer to intellectual forces at play throughout French social thought with which Foucault contends. As an interesting note, though Althusser was Foucault's teacher at the Ecole Normale Supérieure, it is Althusser, not Foucault, who has made public reference to their relationship (Althusser,

For Marx, p. 257). For a discussion of influences on Foucault see Colin Gordon, "Afterword," *P/K*.

32. Foucault, *Archaeology of Knowledge* (*1969a*), pp. 3–10.

33. *Ibid.*, p. 7.

34. Braudel, *The Mediterranean*, vols. 1 and 2.

35. Foucault, *Archaeology of Knowledge* (*1969a*), p. 169.

36. *Ibid.*, pp. 166–67.

37. Emmanuel LeRoy Ladurie, *The Territory of the Historian* (Chicago: University of Chicago Press, 1973), chs. 1–5, and 7.

38. *Ibid.*, p. 111.

39. Foucault, *Archaeology of Knowledge* (*1969a*), pp. 4–5 and 9.

40. "Sur les façons d'écrire l'histoire" (*1967d*), p. 6; and *Order of Things* (*1966a*), part 2.

41. Foucault, *Archaeology of Knowledge* (*1969a*), p. 195.

42. For Bachelard, see inter alia: *Le Nouvel Esprit scientifique* (Paris: Presses Universitairies de France, 1934), *La Formation de l'esprit scientifique: contribution à une psychanalyse de la connaissance objective* (Paris: Vrin, 1938), *The Philosophy of No* (1940; New York: Orion Press, 1968), *Le Rationalisme appliqué* (Paris: Presses Universitaires de France, 1949), *Le Materialisme rational* (Paris: Presses Universitaires de France, 1953). For Canguilhem, see *Études d'histoire et de philosophie des sciences*. For an excellent bibliography of both, see Dominique Lecourt, *Marxism and Epistemology* (London: New Left Books, 1975).

43. Bachelard, *Philosophy of No*, ch. 3. Compare *Le Rationalisme appliqué*, ch. 1.

44. Compare Lecourt, *Marxism and Epistemology*, pp. 8–19.

45. Bachelard, *Le Nouvel Esprit scientifique*, p. 18.

46. Bachelard, *Philosophy of No*, p. 119.

47. Foucault, *Archaeology of Knowledge* (*1969a*), pp. 184–95.

48. *Ibid.*, pp. 187–92.

49. *Ibid.*, p. 187.

50. Compare Foucault, "What is an Author?" (*1969c*), *LCMP*, pp. 131–36.

51. Foucault, "Preface to the English Edition" [1970], *Order of Things* (*1966a*), p. xi.

52. Foucault, *Order of Things* (*1966a*), p. 326.

53. Foucault, *Discourse on Language* (*1971a*), pp. 222–24.

54. Foucault, *Discipline and Punish* (*1975a*), p. 224.

55. For example, see "Theatrum Philosophicum" (*1970d*), *LCMP*, pp. 174–76.

56. Foucault, "Sur les façons d'écrire historie" (1967d), p. 8.

57. Foucault, *Order of Things* (*1966a*), p. 306.

58. *Ibid.*, p. 303.

59. For example, Foucault, *Raymond Roussel* (1963a), pp. 208–10. Compare Foucault's essays: on Bataille, "Preface to Transgression" (*1963c*), *LCMP*, pp. 29–52; on Blanchot, "Language to Infinity" (*1963g*), *LCMP*, pp. 53–67, and "La Pensée du dehors" (1966b); on Hölderin, "The Father's 'No,'" (*1962a*),

LCMP, pp. 68–86; on Flaubert, "Fantasia of the Library" (*1967c*), *LCMP*, pp. 87–109; on Klossowski, "La Prose d'Actéon" (1964a); on Nietzsche, "Nietzsche, Genealogy, History" (*1971d*), *LCMP*, pp. 139–64; and on Nietzsche and Mallarmé, *Order of Things* (*1966a*), pp. 303–97.

60. Foucault, *Archaeology of Knowledge* (*1969a*), p. 119.

61. Foucault, *Order of Things* (*1966a*), p. 306.

62. For example, *ibid.*, p. 328.

63. For an introduction to the importance of Nietzsche in contemporary French thinking, see David Allison, ed., *The New Nietzsche* (New York: Dell, 1977). This collection of essays includes texts by Heidegger, Deleuze, Klossowski, Blanchot, and Derrida. Gilles Deleuze could be said to function for Foucault, like Nietzsche, as a shifter. Deleuze, along with Klossowski, is one contemporary author for whom Foucault has reserved nearly unqualified praise. Foucault began his essay on Deleuze: "I must discuss two books of exceptional merit and importance: *Difference et repetition* and *Logique du sens.* Indeed, these books are so outstanding that they are difficult to discuss . . . I believe that these works will continue to revolve about us in enigmatic resonance with those of Klossowski, another major and excessive sign, and perhaps one day, this century will be known as Deleuzian." See "Theatrum Philosophicum" (*1970d*), *LCMP*, pp. 164–204. For Deleuze on Foucault see "Un Nouvel Archiviste," *Critique* (1970), 274:195–209.

64. Foucault, "Prison Talk," (*1975c*), p. 15.

65. Foucault, "What is an Author?", (*1969c*), *LCMP*, pp. 131–36. On their methods, see Foucault, "Nietzsche, Freud, Marx" (1967a), pp. 190–91.

66. Foucault, *Archaeology of Knowledge* (*1969a*), p. 14; compare pp. 12–14. The concept anthropological sleep is discussed in *Order of Things* (*1966a*), pp. 340–43.

67. Nietzsche, *Thus Spake Zarathustra*, 2:34.

68. Nietzsche, *Genealogy of Morals*, 1:4.

69. *Ibid.*, Preface, p. 6.

70. For a sampling of other discussions of Nietzsche, language, and infinity, see: Maurice Blanchot, *L'Espace littérarie* (Paris: Gallimard, 1955) and *L'Entretien infini* (Paris: Gallimard, 1969); Pierre Klossowski, *Nietzsche et le cercle vicieux* (Paris: Mercure de France, 1969); Gilles Deleuze, *Nietzsche et la philosophie* (Paris: Presses Universitaires de France, 1962) and *Difference et repetition* (Paris: Presses Universitaires de France, 1969); Jacques Derrida, *Spurs, Nietzsche's Styles* (Chicago: University of Chicago Press, 1978).

71. Foucault, "La Pensée du dehors," (1966b), p. 530.

72. Foucault, "Preface to Transgression," (*1963c*), p. 50.

73. See, for example, Roland Barthes, *Sade, Fourier, Loyola* (New York: Hill and Wang, 1976); especially the drawing on p. 147 in the section "The Language Space."

74. Georges Bataille, *Death and Sensuality* (New York: Ballantine 1962), p. 8.

75. *Ibid.*, p. 9.

76. Compare other discussions of difference: Deleuze, *Difference et repetition*, and Derrida, *Writing and Difference*.
77. Bataille, *Death and Sensuality*, pp. 12–13.
78. Compare Foucault, *Discourse on Language*, (*1971a*).
79. Bataille, *Death and Sensuality*, p. 30.
80. The early literary texts are well represented in *LCMP*, parts I and II. Most were published originally between 1962 and 1971.

2. Historical Archaeology

1. Roland Barthes, *Writing Degree Zero* (Boston: Beacon, 1970), pp. 77–78. Compare Foucault, "What is An Author?" (*1969c*).
2. Foucault annoys many for different reasons. We shall not attempt to cataglogue these complaints against his style and method. For a choice sample of the ire he provokes, and his own irksomeness, see his exchange with George Steiner in *Diacritics* (*1971f*) and (*1971g*).
3. Foucault, "Interview" (*1980g*), p. 4.
4. Foucault, "Truth and Power" (*1977a*), p. 297.
5. *Ibid.*
6. *Ibid.*, p. 293.
7. For Foucault's ambivalent relationship to Hegel, see his comments on Jean Hippolyte in *Discourse on Language* (*1971a*), pp. 235–37. For his critical relationship to Althusser, see his, "Sur les façons d'écrire l'histoire" (1967d), p. 6. For his attitudes toward contemporary Marxism generally, see "Truth and Power" (*1977a*).
8. Foucault, *Birth of the Clinic* (*1963b*), ch. 4.
9. *Ibid.*, p. xvii; compare *Archaeology of Knowledge* (*1969a*), *passim*.
10. Foucault, *Archaeology of Knowledge* (*1969a*), p. 119.
11. On the problem of discourse in modern social theory, see Charles Lemert, "Decentered Analysis: Ethnomethodology and Structuralism," *Theory and Society* (1979), 7:298–306.
12. Foucault, *History of Sexuality* (*1976a*), p. 100.
13. Foucault, "History of Systems of Thought" (*1971c*), *LCMP*, p. 200.
14. Foucault, "Nietzsche, Genealogy, History" (*1971d*), *LCMP*, pp. 154–55.
15. Foucault, *History of Sexuality* (*1975a*), p. 98.
16. Dominique Lecourt, *Marxism and Epistemology* (London: New Left Books, 1975), pp. 201–2.
17. For a discussion of similarities and differences between Derrida and Foucault, see Edward Said, "The Problem of Textuality: Two Exemplary Positions," *Critical Inquiry* (1978), 4(4):673–714.
18. Michel Amiot, "Le Relativisme culturaliste de Michel Foucault," *Les Temps Modernes* (1967), 249:1271–98.
19. Foucault, *Archaeology of Knowledge* (*1969a*), pp. 21–30.
20. See, for example, the abrupt note with which Foucault ends and leaves open *Discipline and Punish* (*1975a*), p. 308.

21. Foucault, *Archaeology of Knowledge* (*1969a*), p. 17.

22. *Ibid.*, p. 195.

23. *Ibid.*, p. 15.

24. *Ibid.*, p. 17. Here Foucault explains that the Introduction is partly based on his "Réponse au Cercle d'épistémologie" (1968b). In the same place he also refers to another summary of method for his readers written at the same time, "Réponse à une question" (1968a).

25. Foucault, *Archaeology of Knowledge* (*1969a*), p. 17.

26. "Les Rapports de pouvoir passent à l'intérieur des corps" (1977f), p. 5.

27. Foucault, *Archaeology of Knowledge* (*1969a*), p. 106.

28. *Ibid.*, p. 84.

29. *Ibid.*, pp. 79–87.

30. *Ibid.*, p. 97.

31. *Ibid.*, p. 129.

32. *Ibid.*, p. 127.

33. *Ibid.*, p. 130.

34. *Ibid.*, p. 130.

35. Foucault, *Madness and Civilization* (*1961a*), ch. 9. Compare *Mental Illness and Psychology* (*1954a*).

36. Foucault, *Order of Things* (*1966a*), pp. 386–87.

37. Foucault, *Discipline and Punish* (*1975a*), pp. 307–8.

38. Foucault, *Archaeology of Knowledge* (*1969a*), p. 131.

39. *Ibid.*, p. 74.

40. *Ibid.*, p. 27.

41. *Ibid.*, p. 38.

42. *Ibid.*, p. 46.

43. *Ibid.*, p. 16. Compare "Truth and Power" (*1977a*), p. 296.

44. Foucault, *Archaeology of Knowledge* (*1969a*), p. 45.

45. The following is a general guide to Foucault's many methodological statements: *Archaeology of Knowledge* (*1969a*); "Réponse à une question" (1968a); "Réponse au Cercle d'épistémologie" (1968b); "Preface," *Birth of the Clinic* (*1963b*); "Foreword to the English Edition," *Order of Things* (*1966a*); "Nietzsche, Genealogy, History" (*1971d*); *Discipline and Punish* (*1975a*), pp. 23–25; *History of Sexuality* (*1976a*), part 4; "Two Lectures" (*1976f*), *P/K*.

3. Power-Knowledge and Discourse

1. Foucault, "Power and Sex" (*1977g*), p. 159.

2. Foucault, "Truth and Power" (*1977a*), p. 293. This, quite intentionally, involves a spatial image. On the close connection between spatializing discourse, knowledge, and the analysis of power, see Foucault, "Questions on Geography," (*1976g*), *P/K*, pp. 63–77, where Foucault writes (on pp. 70–71): "For all those who confuse history with the old schemas of evolution, living continuity, organic development, the progress of consciousness or the

project of existence, the use of spatial terms seems to have the air of an anti-history. If one started to talk in terms of space that meant one was hostile to time. It meant, as the fools say, that one 'denied history' that one was a 'technocrat.' They didn't understand that to trace the forms of implantation, delimitation and demarcation of domains meant the throwing into relief of processes—historical ones, needless to say—of power. The spatializing description of discursive realities gives on to the analysis of related effects of power." Translation slightly altered.

3. Foucault, "Truth and Power" (*1977a*), p. 298. Compare "Two Lectures" (1976f), *P/K*, pp. 80–83, 93.

4. Foucault, "Truth and Power" (*1977a*), p. 300. Compare "Two Lectures" (1976f), *P/K*, p. 90.

5. Foucault, *Birth of the Clinic* (*1963b*), p. 16.

6. Foucault, *Discourse on Language* (*1971a*), p. 216.

7. *Ibid.*, pp. 216–24.

8. *Ibid.*, p. 219.

9. Foucault, "Power and Sex" (*1977g*), p. 153.

10. Foucault, *Discourse on Language* (*1971a*), p. 220.

11. *Ibid.*, p. 220. In 1976 Foucault offered a clarification of the distinction between archaeology and genealogy. In "Two Lectures" (*1976f*), p. 85, he said: "If we were to characterize it in two terms, then 'archaeology' would be the appropriate methodology of this analysis of local discursivities, and 'genealogy' would be the tactics whereby, on the basis of the descriptions of these local discursivities, the subjected knowledges which were thus released would be brought into play." It is hard to tell whether this is a retrospective adjustment in Foucault's vocabulary or a reflection of the fact that, after *The Archaeology of Knowledge* (*1969a*), his main studies—*Discipline and Punish* (*1975a*) and *History of Sexuality* (*1976a*)—were indeed more regional and explicitly political, hence genealogical. In any case, we hold the view that genealogy is basic, and that the distinction appears to be spurious.

12. Foucault, "A Preface to Transgression" (*1963c*), *LCMP*, pp. 30–31.

13. *Ibid.*, p. 32.

14. *Ibid.*, p. 36.

15. *Ibid.*, p. 38.

16. Foucault, *The Order of Things* (*1966a*) p. 314.

17. *Ibid.*, p. 315.

18. *Ibid.*, pp. 340–43. Anthropology in Foucault's works refers not to the academic discipline of that name, but to the "analytic of man" described in *The Order of Things* (*1966a*). Anthropological thought is the discursive formation characteristic of Western modernity that makes Man the object and subject of knowledge.

19. Foucault, "A Preface to Transgression" (*1963c*), p. 50.

20. Foucault, "Nietzsche, Genealogy, History" (*1971d*), *LCMP*, p. 148.

21. *Ibid.*, p. 26.

22. Foucault, *Discipline and Punish* (*1975a*), p. 24.

23. *Ibid.*, p. 26.

24. *Ibid.*, pp. 220–21.

25. *Ibid.*, p. 25.

26. *Ibid.*, p. 26.

27. *Ibid.*, p. 28. For the same conception expressed in other terms, see: Foucault, "Body/Power" (*1975d*), *P/K*, p. 55: "I believe the great fantasy is the idea of a social body constituted by the universality of wills. Now the phenomenon of the social body is the effect not of a consensus but of the materiality of power operating on the very bodies of individuals."

28. Foucault, *Discipline and Punish* (*1975a*), p. 29.

29. *Ibid.*, p. 29.

30. *Ibid.*, p. 193.

31. Foucault, *The History of Sexuality* (*1976a*), p. 49.

32. *Ibid.*, p. 123.

33. *Ibid.*, pp. 104–5.

34. *Ibid.*, pp. 105–6. In "Confession of the Flesh" (*1977i*), *P/K*, pp. 194–95, Foucault amplifies this definition: "What I'm trying to pick out with this term is, firstly, a thoroughly heterogeneous ensemble consisting of discourses, institutions, architectural forms, regulatory decisions, laws, administrative measures, scientific statements, philosophical, moral and philanthropic propositions—in short, the said as much as the unsaid. Such are the elements of the apparatus. The apparatus itself is the system of relationships that can be established between these elements. Secondly, what I am trying to identify in this apparatus is precisely the nature of the connection that can exist between these heterogeneous elements. Thus, a particular discourse can figure at one time as the programme of an institution, and at another it can function as a means of justifying or masking a practice which itself remains silent, or as a secondary re-interpretation of this practice, opening out for it a new field of rationality." "Apparatus of sexuality" here refers to what we have translated as "affective mechanism of sexuality"; see Concepts Used by Foucault.

35. Foucault, *History of Sexuality* (*1976a*), p. 82. Compare the discussions of power and power and sovereignty and right in the West in "Two Lectures" (*1976f*), *P/K*, pp. 95–96, and in "Power and Strategies" (*1977h*), *P/K*, pp. 139–43.

36. Foucault, *History of Sexuality* (*1976a*), pp. 89–90. Compare Foucault's observation in "The History of Sexuality," (*1977f*), *P/K*, p. 186.

37. Foucault, *History of Sexuality* (*1976a*), p. 82. Translation altered.

38. *Ibid.*, p. 123.

39. *Ibid.*, p. 128.

40. *Ibid.*, p. 129.

41. *Ibid.*, p. 136. Translation altered.

42. *Ibid.*, p. 137.

43. *Ibid.*, p. 139.

44. *Ibid.*, p. 141.

45. Foucault, *Folie et déraison. Histoire de la folie à l'âge classique* (1961a), 2nd ed., pp. 535–47.

46. Foucault, *History of Sexuality* (*1976a*), p. 143.

47. *Ibid.*, p. 145.

48. *Ibid.*, pp. 151–52. *Dispositif* generally refers to the internal workings of a machine, such as a drive gear. Consequently, we have translated *dispositif de sexualité* as "affective mechanisms of sexuality." In addition to being more literal than "deployment of sexuality" in the standard English translation, affective mechanism also conveys the possible allusion on Foucault's part to the theory of desiring machines in Deleuze and Guattari's *Anti-Oedipus* (New York: Viking Press, 1977). The translation has been so altered.

49. Foucault, *History of Sexuality* (*1976a*), pp. 154–55.

50. *Ibid.*, p. 154.

51. Foucault, *Madness and Civilization* (*1961a*), p. 24.

52. Foucault, "Interview" (*1980g*), p. 5. Along the same lines, Foucault says in "The History of Sexuality" (*1977f*), *P/K*, p. 193: "As to the problem of fiction, it seems to me to be a very important one; I am well aware that I have never written anything but fictions. I do not mean to say, however, that truth is therefore absent. It seems to me that the possibility exists for fiction to function in truth, for a fictional discourse to induce effects of truth, and for bringing it about that a true discourse engenders or 'manufactures' something that does not as yet exist, that is, 'fictions' it. One 'fictions' history on the basis of a political reality that makes it true."

53. Foucault, "Intellectuals and Power" (*1972f*), *LCMP*, p. 208. On the political goal of history, see his "Questions on Geography" (*1976g*), *P/K*, pp. 64–65.

54. Foucault, "Intellectuals and Power" (*1972f*), *LCMP*, pp. 207–8. On the role of theory and power, see his "Power and Strategies" (*1977h*), *P/K*, p. 145.

55. Foucault, "Truth and Power" (*1977a*), pp. 304–7.

56. *Ibid.*, p. 302–4.

57. *Ibid.*, p. 304.

58. Foucault, *History of Sexuality* (*1976a*), p. 137.

59. *Ibid.*, p. 157. Compare the concept of the plebs in "Power and Strategies" (*1977h*), *P/K*, pp. 137–38: "The plebs is no doubt not a real sociological entity. But there is indeed always something in the social body, in classes, groups and individuals themselves which in some sense escapes relations of power, something which is by no means a more or less docile or reactive primal matter, but rather a centrifugal movement, an inverse energy, a discharge. There is certainly no such thing as 'the' plebs; rather there is, as it were, a certain plebeian quality or aspect ('*de la' plèbe*). There is plebs in bodies, in souls, in individuals, in the proletariat, in the bourgeoisie, but everywhere in a diversity of forms and extensions, of energies and irreducibilities."

60. Foucault, "Revolutionary Action: 'Until Now'" (*1971i*), *LCMP*, pp. 221–22.

61. Foucault, "Preface" (*1977c*), *Anti-Oedipus*, pp. xiii–xiv.
62. Foucault, "Revolutionary Action: 'Until Now'" (*1971i*), *LCMP*, p. 228.

4. Limits and Social Theory

1. On the general question of the contradictions in social theory, see Alvin Gouldner's trilogy *The Dark Side of the Dialectic*, especially *The Two Marxisms: Contradictions and Anomalies in the Development of Theory* (New York: Seabury, 1980). Compare Foucault, *Archaeology of Knowledge* (*1969a*), 184–86.

2. For an extensive discussion of Annales historiography see Traian Stoianovich, *French Historical Method: The Annales Paradigm* (Ithaca, N.Y.: Cornell University Press, 1976). A very fine treatment is also to be found in Georg G. Iggers, *New Directions in European Historiography* (Middletown, Conn.: Wesleyan University Press, 1975). The most comprehensive introduction is Jean Glenisson, "L'Historiographie française contemporaine: tendances et realisations," *La Recherche historique en France de 1940 à 1965*, Comité Français des Sciences Historiques (Paris: Editions du Centre National de la Recherche Scientifique, 1965), pp. ix–lxiv.

3. Stoianovich, *French Historical Method*, p. 65.

4. Lucien Febvre, *A Geographical Introduction to History*, E. G. Mountford and J. H. Paxton, trans. (New York: Knopf, 1925), pp. 241–45.

5. See Stoianovich, *French Historical Method*. Foucault discusses these questions in "Questions on Geography" (*1976g*), *P/K*, pp. 63–77. Also see the importance of the analysis of space as a counterfoil to the retreat of philosophy into the concept of time in Foucault, "The Eye of Power" (*1977b*), *P/K*, pp. 149–51.

6. Fernand Braudel, "Histoire et sciences sociales: la longue durée," *Écrits sur l'histoire* (Paris: Flammarion, 1969), pp. 41–83.

7. Foucault, *Archaeology of Knowledge* (*1969a*) p. 9; and "La Poussière et le nuage" (1980b), p. 34.

8. Foucault, *Birth of the Clinic* (*1963b*), p. 16; *Archaeology of Knowledge* (*1969a*), p. 45; and *History of Sexuality* (*1976a*), p. 200.

9. Foucault, *Archaeology of Knowledge* (*1969a*), p. 227–28.

10. *Ibid.*, p. 6.

11. *Ibid.*, p. 7.

12. *Ibid.*, p. 11.

13. Jacques Lacan, *Écrits: A Selection*, Alan Sheridan, trans. (New York: Norton, 1977), pp. 85, 285, 299.

14. *Ibid.*, p. 299.

15. *Ibid.*, pp. 310, 140–41.

16. Julia Kristeva, "La Semiologie: science critique et/ou critique de la science," *Théorie d'ensemble* (Paris: Editions du Seuil, 1968), pp. 87 and 89.

17. Julia Kristeva, *La Révolution du langage poétique* (Paris: Éditions du Seuil, 1974), p. 188.

18. Foucault, *Order of Things* (*1966a*), pp. 273–376; and *Madness and Civilization* (*1961a*), pp. 221–28; compare pp. 269–78.

19. Foucault, *Order of Things* (*1966a*), p. xiv.

20. Theodor W. Adorno, *Negative Dialectics*, E. B. Ashton, trans. (New York: Seabury, 1973), p. xx.

21. Jürgen Habermas, *Knowledge and Human Interests*, Jeremy J. Shapiro, trans. (Boston: Beacon Press, 1971), pp. 274–300.

22. Adorno, *Negative Dialectics*, p. 185; Adorno and Horkheimer, *Dialectic of Enlightenment* (New York: Seabury 1972).

23. Adorno, *Negative Dialectics*, pp. 183–85.

24. Habermas, *Knowledge and Human Interests*, pp. 246–72.

25. Habermas, "Toward a Theory of Communicative Competence," in Hans Peter Dreitzel, *Recent Sociology, No. 2*, Patterns of Communicative Behavior (New York: Macmillan, 1970), pp. 115–58. Compare Habermas, *Communication and the Evolution of Society* (Boston: Beacon Press, 1979).

26. Foucault, *The Order of Things* (*1966a*), pp. 340–41.

27. *Ibid.*, p. 342.

28. Foucault, "Intellectuals and Power" (*1972f*), *LCMP*, p. 213.

29. Foucault, *Discipline and Punish* (*1975a*), pp. 257–92. See also Foucault's discussion in "Prison Talk" (*1975c*), *P/K*, p. 39. Power is not primarily hierarchical, but capillary.

30. Foucault, *Discipline and Punish* (*1975a*), p. 256.

31. Foucault, *History of Sexuality* (*1976a*), pp. 120–27. Quotation on p. 127.

32. Foucault, "Truth and Power" (*1977a*), p. 306.

33. In *Archaeology of Knowledge* (*1969a*), pp. 114–15, Foucault hedges somewhat while affirming this goal: "Rather than *founding* a theory—and perhaps being able to do so (I do not deny that I regret not yet having succeeded in doing so)—my present concern is to *establish* a possibility." Whatever secret ambitions are hidden in the quadruple (!) negative in the parenthetical clause, it remains that Foucault has not, since *Archaeology of Knowledge*, sought to found a theoretically formal science.

34. Foucault, *Archaeology of Knowledge* (*1969a*), pp. 175–95.

35. *Ibid.*, p. 186.

36. *Ibid.*, p. 194. Compare "Prison Talk" (*1975c*), pp. 51–52.

37. Foucault, "Truth and Power" (*1977a*), pp. 305–6.

38. For example, Louis Althusser, "Contradiction and Overdetermination," in *For Marx* (1962; New York, Vintage Books, 1970); and Nicos Poulantzas, *Political Power and Social Class* (1968; London: New Left Books, 1975).

39. Jürgen Habermas, *Legitimation Crisis* (Boston: Beacon Press, 1975); and Claus Offe, "Political Authority and Class Structures—An Analysis of Late Capitalist Societies," *International Journal of Sociology* (Spring 1972), 2(1): 73–108; and Offe, "Structural Problems of the Capitalist State," in *German Political Studies*, vol. 1, Klaus von Beyme, ed. (London: Sage Publications, 1974).

40. Theda Skocpol, *States and Social Revolutions* (Cambridge: Cambridge University Press, 1979), p. 33.

41. In *Order of Things* (*1966a*), pp. xii–xxii, Foucault admits that change, along with causality and the subject, is a gap in his studies. He may have corrected somewhat the latter two problems in subsequent works, but change remains an open question. See, however, the beginnings of an answer in *Archaeology of Knowledge* (*1969a*), pp. 166–76.

42. For example, Foucault, "Sur les façons d'écrire l'histoire," (1967d), p. 6.

43. See, for example André Glucksmann, "A Ventriloquist Structuralism," *New Left Review* (March–April 1972), 72; Frank Parkin, *Marxism and Class Theory: A Bourgeois Critique* (New York: Columbia University Press, 1979), p. 154 *et passim.*; E. P. Thompson, *The Poverty of Theory and Other Essays* (New York and London: Monthly Review Press, 1978), ch. 1.

44. Nicos Poultantzas, *Classes in Contemporary Capitalism* (London: New Left Books, 1975).

45. Poultanzas, "The Capitalist State: A Reply to Miliband and Laclau," *New Left Review*, (1976), no. 95, pp. 63–83.

46. Parkin, *Marxism and Class Theory*, especially ch. 2.

47. Anthony Giddens, Review of Parkin, *Marxism and Class Theory*, in *Theory and Society* (1980), 9:877–90.

48. Just one recent example that includes, in chapter 1, a summary of current literature is G. William Domhoff, *The Powers That Be* (New York: Vintage, 1978). Compare Alvin W. Gouldner *The Dialectic of Ideology and Technology* (New York: Seabury, 1976) and *The Future of Intellectuals and the Rise of the New Class* (New York: Seabury, 1978); and George Konrad and Ivan Szelenyi, *The Intellectuals on the Road to Class Power* (New York: Harcourt Brace and Jovanovich, 1979).

49. For example, see Alain Touraine, *The Voice and the Eye* (Cambridge: Cambridge University Press; Paris: Maison des Sciences de l'Homme, 1981) and Touraine, *The Post Industrial Society* (New York: Random House, 1971). Compare George Ross, "Marxism and the New Middle Class," *Theory and Society* (March 1978), 5(2):163–90.

50. Karl Marx, "Introduction," *Grundrisse* (1857; London: New Left Books, 1974).

51. Perry Anderson, *Considerations on Western Marxism* (London: New Left Books, 1976), especially pp. 109–21.

52. For example, Immanuel Wallerstein, *The Capitalist World-Economy* (Cambridge: Cambridge University Press; Paris: Maison des Sciences de l'Homme, 1979).

53. See, for example, the contributions of Wallerstein, Braudel, and Hobsbawm and others in *Review* (Winter/Spring 1978), vol. 1, nos. 3 and 4.

54. Wallerstein, *Capitalist World-Economy*, pp. vii–xii and pp. 152–64.

55. Habermas, *Knowledge and Human Interests*, "Toward a Theory of Communicative Competence." Compare Charles Lemert, *Sociology and the Twilight of Man* (Carbondale: Southern Illinois University Press, 1979), ch. 8.

56. Harold Garfinkel and Harvey Sacks, "On Formal Structures of Prac-

tical Actions," in John McKinney and Edward Tiryakian, eds., *Theoretical Sociology* (New York: Appleton-Century-Crofts, 1970), pp. 337–66; and Aaron Cicourel, *Cognitive Sociology* (New York: Macmillan, 1974).

57. For example, Pierre Bourdieu, *Outline of a Theory of Practice* (Cambridge: Cambridge University Press, 1977), and *Le Sens pratique* (Paris: Minuit, 1980).

58. Touraine, *The Voice and the Eye*; and Anthony Giddens, *Central Problems in Social Theory* (London: Macmillan, 1979).

59. Foucault, *Order of Things* (*1966a*), p. 343.

Foucault's Publications

This list of books, articles, interviews, prefaces, introductions, comments, and reviews published through 1980 is comprehensive except for the omission of several relatively minor pieces. Readers may wish to consult sources which, in these few instances, supplement this list. These same sources were occasionally helpful in checking our own entries:

> Bouchard, Donald, ed. *Language, Counter-Memory, and Practice: Selected Essays and Interviews by Michel Foucault.* Ithaca, N.Y.: Cornell University Press, 1977. Cited as *LCMP* below.
>
> Gordon, Colin, ed. *Power/Knowledge: Selected Interviews and Other Writings, 1972–1977, by Michel Foucault.* New York: Pantheon/Random House, 1980. Cited as *P/K* below.
>
> Morris, Meaghan, and Paul Patton, ed. *Michel Foucault: Power, Truth, and Strategy.* Sydney: Feral Publications, 1979. Cited as *PTS* below.
>
> [Editors.] *Magazine littéraire* (juin 1975), 101:6–33.

To display the chronological sequence of Foucault's work and to cross-reference translations to the originals, the year of original publication is given in the left column. Entries are organized chronologically with letter notations used to discriminate publications occurring in the same year. Dates in roman type signify originals; italicized dates refer to translations.

1954a   *Maladie mentale et personnalité.* [Revised, retitled edition in 1962 as *Maladie mentale et psychologie.*] Paris: Presses Universitaires de France.

1954a   *Mental Illness and Psychology.* Translated by Alan Sheridan. New York: Harper & Row, 1976.

1954b   "Introduction" [to and translation of] *Le Rêve et l'existence,* by Ludwig Binswanger. Paris: Desclée de Brouwer.

1961a   *Folie et déraison: Histoire de la folie à l'âge classique.* Paris: Plon;

abridged edition, 1962; second edition, Paris: Gallimard, 1972.

1961a *Madness and Civilization: A History of Insanity in the Age of Reason.* Translated by Richard Howard. [Translation of the 1962 abridged edition with supplements from the original, 1961a.] New York: Random House, 1965.

1962a "Le 'non' du père." *Critique,* 178:195–209.

1962a "The Father's 'No,'" In *LCMP* (1977).

1962b "Un si cruel savoir." *Critique,* 182:597–611.

1962c "Dire et voire chez Raymond Roussel." *Lettre Ouverte* (été), 4:38–51.

1962d "Preface." *Rousseau juge de Jean-Jacques,* by J.-J. Rousseau, Paris: A. Colin.

1963a *Raymond Roussel.* Paris: Gallimard.

1963b *Naissance de la clinique: Une archéologie du regard médical.* Paris: Presses Universitaires de France; revised edition, 1972.

1963b *The Birth of the Clinic: An Archaeology of Medical Perception.* Translated by A. M. Sheridan Smith. New York: Random House, 1975.

1963c "Preface à la transgression." *Critique,* 195–96:751–70.

1963c "A Preface to Transgression." In *LCMP* (1977).

1963d "Distance, aspect, origine." *Critique,* 198:931–46. Reprinted in *Tel Quel, Théorie d'ensemble,* pp. 11–23. Paris: Seuil, 1968.

1963e "La Metamorphosé et le labyrinthe." *Nouvelle Revue Française* (avril 1963), 124:638–61.

1963f "Guetter le jour qui vient." *Nouvelle Revue Française* (octobre 1963), 130:709–16.

1963g "La Langage à l'infini." *Tel Quel,* 15:44–53.

1963g "Language to Infinity." In *LCMP* (1977).

1964a "La Prose d'Actéon." *Nouvelle Revue Française* (mars 1964), 135:444–59.

1964b "Le Langage de l'espace." *Critique* (avril 1964), 203:378–82.

1964c "Le Mallarmé de J.-P. Richard." *Annales, Economies, Sociétés, Civilizations* (avril 1964), 5:996–1004.

1964d "Pourquoi réédite-t-on Raymond Roussel? Un Precurseur de nôtre littérature moderne." *Le Monde* (22 âout 1964), 6,097:9.

1964e "Debats sur le roman." [Discussion.] *Tel Quel* (printemps 1964), 17:13–54.

1964f "Debat sur la poésie." [Discussion.] *Tel Quel* (printemps 1964), 17:69–82.

1964g "Nerval est-il le plus grande poète de XIX siècle?" *Arts* (11 novembre 1964).

1966a   *Les Mots et les choses. Une Archéologie des sciences humaines.* Paris: Gallimard.

1966a   *The Order of Things: An Archaeology of the Human Sciences.* New York: Random House, 1970.

1966b   "La Pensée du dehors." *Critique*, 229:523–46.

1966c   "L'Arrière-Fable." *L'Arc*, 29:5–12.

1966d   "La Prose du monde." *Diogene*, 53:20–41.

1966e   "L'Homme est-il mort?" [Interview.] *Arts-Loisirs* (15 juin 1966), 38:9.

1966f   "Entretien." [Interview with Madeleine Chapsal on *Les Mots et les choses.*] *La Quinzaine Littéraire* (16 mai 1966), 5:13–14.

1966g   "Entretien." [Interview with Raymond Bellour on *Les Mots et les choses.*] *Les Lettres Françaises* (31 mars 1966), 1,123:3–4. Also in *Le Livre des autres*, pp. 135–44. Edited by Raymond Bellour. Paris: L'Herne, n.d.

1967a   "Nietzsche, Freud, Marx." In *Nietzsche*, pp. 183–97. Paris: Cahiers de Royaumont/Minuit.

1967b   Preface [with Gilles Deleuze]. *Oeuvres philisophiques complètes. Le gai savoir. Les fragments posthummes (1881–1882)*, by Fredrick Nietzsche. Paris.

1967c   "Un 'fantastique' de bibliothèque." In *Cahiers de la Compagnie Renaud-Barrault* (mars 1967), 59:7–30.

1967c   "Fantasia of the Library." In *LCMP* (1977).

1967d   "Sur les façons d'écrire l'histoire." [Interview with Raymond Bellour.] *Les Lettres Françaises* (15 juin 1967), 1,187:6–9. Also in *Le Livre des autres*, pp. 189–207. Edited by Raymond Bellour. Paris: Seuil, n.d.

1968a   "Réponse à une question." *Esprit* (mai 1968), 5:851–74.

1968a   "History, Discourse and Discontinuity." Translated by Anthony M. Nazzaro. *Salmagundi* (Summer/Fall 1972), 20:225–48.

1968b   "Réponse au Cercle d'épistémologie. Sur l'archéologie des sciences." *Cahiers pour L'Analyse*, 9:5–40.

1968b   "On the Archaeology of the Sciences." [Abridged.] *Theoretical Practice* (1971), 3–4:108–27.

1968c   "Ceci n'est pas une pipe." *Les Cahiers du Chemin* (1968), vol. 2.

1968d   "Correspondance à propos des *Entretiens sur Foucault.*" *Pensée* (juin 1968), 139:114–17.

1968e   "Foucault répond à Sartre." [Interview with Jean-Pierre El Kabbach.] *La Quinzaine Littéraire* (1 mars 1968), 46:20–22.

1969a   *L'Archéologie du savoir.* Paris: Gallimard.

1969a   *The Archaeology of Knowledge.* Translated by A. M. Sheridan Smith. New York: Random House/Pantheon, 1972.

1969b   "Preface." *Grammaire générale et raisonée*, by Arnauld and Lancelot. Paris: Républications Paulet.

1969c   "Qu'est-ce qu'un auteur?" *Bulletin de la Société Française de Philosophie*, 63(3):73–104. [Includes a discussion, following.]

1969c   "What is an Author?" In *LCMP* (1977). Also in *Partisan Review* (1975), 42(4):603–14.

1969d   "Ariane s'est pendue." Review of *Logique du sens*, by Gilles Deleuze. *Nouvel Observateur* (31 mars 1969), 229:36–37.

1969e   "Jean Hippolyte (1907–1968)." *Revue de Métaphysique et Morale*, 74.

1969f   "Entretien." [Interview with Jean-Jacques Brochier on *Archéologie du savoir*.] *Magazine Littéraire* (avril-mai 1969), 28:23–25.

1970a   "Il y aura scandale, mais . . ." *Nouvel Observateur* (7 septembre 1970), 304:40.

1970b   "Croître et multiplier." Review of *La Logique du vivant*, by Francois Jacob. *Le Monde* (15–16 novembre 1970), 8,037:13.

1970c   "La Situation de Cuvier dans l'histoire de la biologie." *Revue d'Histoire des Sciences*, 23:63–69.

1970c   "Cuvier's Position in the History of Biology." *Critique of Anthropology* (1979), 4:125–30.

1970d   "Theatrum Philosophicum." On *Difference et repetition* and *Logique de sens*, by Gilles Deleuze. *Critique*, 282:885–909.

1970d   "Theatrum Philosophicum." In *LCMP* (1977).

1970e   "Preface." *Oeuvres*, by Georges Bataille. Paris: Gallimard.

1970f   "Preface." *La Logique grammaire*, by Jean Pierre Brisset. Paris: Tchou.

1971a   *L'Ordre du discours*. Leçon inaugural au Collège de France prononcée le 2 decembre 1970. Paris: Gallimard.

1971a   *The Discourse on Language*. Translated by Rupert Swyer. [Printed as an appendix to *Archaeology of Knowledge*.] New York: Random House, 1972.

1971b   "Le Discours de Toul." *Le Nouvel Observateur* (27 decembre 1971), vol. 372.

1971c   "Histoire de systèmes deç pensées." *Annuaire de Collège de France*. Paris: Collège de France.

1971c   "History of Systems of Thought." In *LCMP* (1977).

1971d   "Nietzsche, la genéalogie, l'histoire." In *Hommage à Jean Hyppolite*, pp. 145–72. Paris: Presses Universitaires de France.

1971d   "Nietzsche, Genealogy, History." In *LCMP* (1977).

1971e   Preface. *La Tentation de Sainte Antoine*, by Gustave Flaubert. Paris: Gallimard.

1971f   "Monstrosities in Criticism." [On George Steiner.] *Diacritics* (Fall), 1:57–60.

1971g   "Response [to George Steiner]." *Diacritics* (Winter), 1:59–61.

1971h   "Lettre de Foucault." *Pensée*, 159:141–44.

1971i   "Par delà le bien et le mal." [Discussion with students.] *Actuel* (novembre 1971), 14:42–47. Version in *C'est demain la veille*, pp. 19–43. Paris: Seuil, 1973.

1971i   "Revolutionary Action: Until Now." [Discussion.] In *LCMP* (1977).

1972a   "La Folie, l'absence, d'oeuvre." *La Table Ronde* (mai 1964). Reprinted in *Histoire de la folie à l'âge classique*, pp. 575–82. Second edition. Paris: Gallimard.

1972b   "Bachelard, le philosophe et son ombre . . ." *Le Figaro Littéraire* (30 septembre 1972), vol. 1376.

1972c   "Les Deux Morts de Pompidou." *Le Nouvel Observateur* (4 decembre 1972), vol. 421.

1972d   "Mon Corps, ce papier, ce feu." [Response to Jacques Derrida.] In *Histoire de la folie à l'âge classique*, pp. 583–603. Second edition. Paris: Gallimard.

1972d   "My Body, This Paper, This Fire." *Oxford Literary Review* (Autumn 1979), 4:5–28.

1972e   "Sur la justice populaire: Debat avec les Maos." *Les Temps Modernes* (1972), vol. 310 bis.

1972e   "On Popular Justice: A Discussion with Maoists." In *P/K* (1980).

1972f   "Intellectuels et pouvoir." [Discussion with Gilles Deleuze.] *L'Arc*, 49:3–16.

1972f   "Intellectuals and Power." [Discussion with Gilles Deleuze.] Translated by M. Seem. *Telos*, 16:103–9. Also in *LCMP* (1977).

1972g   "Table ronde." [Discussion.] *Esprit*, 4:678–703.

1973a   *Ceci n'est pas une pipe.* Montpellier: Fata Morgana. [Originally published as an article in *Les Cahiers du Chemin* (1968), vol. 2.]

1973b   *Moi, Pierre Rivière, ayant égorgé ma mère, ma soeur et mon frère . . . Un cas de parricide au XIXe siècle.* [Collaborative work.] Paris: Gallimard.

1973b   *I, Pierre Riviere, Having Slaughtered My Mother, My Sister, and My Brother . . . A Case of Parricide in the 19th Century.* Translated by F. Jellinek. New York: Random House, 1975.

1974a   "On Attica." [Interview with John K. Simon.] *Telos*, 19:154–61.

1975a   *Surveiller et punir. Naissance de la prison.* Paris: Gallimard.

1975a   *Discipline and Punish: The Birth of the Prison.* Translated by Alan Sheridan. New York: Random House, 1977.

1975b   "Des supplice aux cellules." [Interview with R. P. Droit on *Surveiller et punir.*] *Le Monde* (21 février 1975), p. 16.

1975c   "Entretien sur la prison: Le libre et sa methode." [Interview with J. J. Brochier on *Surveiller et punir.*] *Magazine Littéraire* (juin 1975), 101:27–33. Also in *Politiques de la philosophie.* Edited by Dominique Grisoni. Paris: Grasset, 1976.

1975c   "Prison Talk." [Interview.] Translated by Colin Gordon. *Radical Philosophy* (1977), 16:10–15. Also in *P/K* (1980).

1975d   "Pouvoir et corps." *Quel Corps?* (21 septembre–octobre 1975). [Interview with the editors.]

1975d   "Body/Power." [Interview with the editors of *Quel Corps?*] In *P/K* (1980).

1976a   *Histoire de la sexualité, I: La Volonté de savoir.* Paris: Gallimard.

1976a   *The History of Sexuality, vol. 1: An Introduction.* Translated by Robert Hurley. New York: Random House, 1978.

1976b   *Les Machines à guerir. Aux origines de l'hôpital moderne.* Paris: Institut de l'environnement. [Collaborative work.]

1976c   "L'Occident et la verité du sexe." *Le Monde* (5–6 novembre 1976), p. 24.

1976c   "The West and the Truth of Sex." *Sub/stance* (1978), vol. 20.

1976d   "La Fonction politique de l'intellectuel." *Politique Hebdo* (29 novembre 1976), 247:31–33. [Abridged version of 1977a.]

1976d   "The Political Function of the Intellectual." [Abridged version of 1977a.] Translated by Colin Gordon. *Radical Philosophy,* 17:12–14.

1976e   "La Politique de la santé au XVIIIe siècle." In *Les Machines à guerir. Aux origines de l'hôpital moderne,* by Michel Foucault et al. Paris: Institut de l'Environnnment.

1976e   "The Politics of Health in the Eighteenth Century." In *P/K* (1980).

1976f   "Two Lectures." [January 7, 1976, and January 14, 1976.] In *P/K* (1980). Appeared also in Italian in Michel Foucault, *Microfisica del Potere.* Turin, Einaudi: 1977.

1976g   "Questions à Michel Foucault sur la geographie." [Interview with editors.] *Hérodote* (janvier–mars 1976), vol. 1.

1976g   "Questions on Geography." In *P/K* (1980).

1976h   "Crimes et châtiments en U.R.S.S. et ailleurs . . ." [Interview with K. S. Karol.] *Le Nouvel Observateur* (26 janvier 1976), 582:34–37.

1976h   "The Politics of Crime." [Abridged.] Translated by Mollie Horowitz. *Partisan Review* (Fall 1976), 43:453–59.

(1977) *Language, Counter-memory, and Practice: Selected Essays and Interviews.* Edited by Donald Bouchard. Ithaca, N.Y.: Cornell University Press, 1977. Cited as *LCMP.*

1977a "Verité et pouvoir." [Interview.] *L'Arc,* 70:16–22. Abridgement of an interview with Alexandra Fontana published in Italian in Michel Foucault, *Microfisica del Potere.* Turin: Einaudi, 1977.

1977a "Truth and Power." [Interview.] Translated by Garth Gillan. In *French Sociology,* pp. 293–307. Edited by Charles Lemert, New York: Columbia University Press, 1981. Other translations: by Felicity Edholm in *Critique of Anthropology,* 4(13/14):131–38, [abridged]; in *PTS* (1979); and *P/K* (1980).

1977b "L'Oeil du pouvoir." [Discussion with Michelle Perrot and Jean-Pierre Barrou.] In *Le Panoptique,* by Jeremy Bentham. Paris: Pierre Belfund, 1977.

1977b "The Eye of Power." *Semiotexte* (1978), 3(2):6–19. Also in *P/K* (1980).

1977c "Preface." *Anti-Oedipus: Capitalism and Schizophrenia,* by Gilles Deleuze and Felix Guattari. New York: Viking Press.

1977d "La Vie des hommes infâmes." *Cahiers du Chemin* (15 janvier 1977), 29:13–29.

1977d "The Life of Infamous Men." In *PTS* (1980).

1977e "Le Supplice de la vérité." *Chemin de Ronde. La Torture* (1977), 1:162–63.

1977f "Les Rapports de pouvoir passent à l'interieur des corps." [Interview with Lucette Finas on *Histoire de la sexualité, I.*] *La Quinzaine Littéraire* (1–15 janvier 1977), 247:4–6.

1977f "The History of Sexuality." [Interview.] In *PTS* (1979) and in *P/K* (1980).

1977g "Non au sexe roi." [Interview with Bernard-Henri Lévy on *Histoire de la sexualité, I.*] *Le Nouvel Observateur* (12 mars 1977), vol. 644.

1977g "Power and Sex." Translated by David J. Parent. *Telos* (1977), 32:152–61. Also: "The History of Sexuality: Interview." Translated by Geoff Bennington. *Oxford Literary Review* (1980), 4(2):3–14.

1977h "Pouvoirs et stratégies." [Interview with editors.] *Les Révoltes Logiques* (1977), vol. 4.

1977h "Power and Strategies." [Interview with the editors of *Les Révoltes Logiques.*] In *PTS* (1979) and *P/K* (1980).

1977i "Le Jeu de Michel Foucault." [Interview with editors.] *Ornicar?* (juillet 1977), vol. 10.

1977i "The Confession of the Flesh." [Interview.] In *P/K* (1980).

1977j   "Enferment, psychiatrie, prison." [Discussion with David Cooper and others.] *Change* (octobre 1977), 32–33:76–110. Extract in *La Quinzaine Littéraire* (16 octobre 1977), vol. 265.

(1979)   *Power, Truth, and Strategy.* Edited by Meaghan Morris and Paul Patton. Sydney: Feral Publications, 1979. Cited as *PTS*.

1979a   "Lettre ouverte à Mehdi Bazargan." *Le Nouvel Observateur* (9 avril 1979), vol. 752.

(1980)   *Power/Knowledge: Selected Interviews and Other Writings, 1972–1977.* Edited by Colin Gordon. New York: Pantheon/ Random House, 1980. Cited as *P/K*.

1980a   *L'Impossible Prison.* [Collaborative work.] Paris: Seuil.

1980b   "La Poussière et le nuage." In *L'Impossible Prison*, pp. 29–39. [Collaborative work.] Paris: Seuil.

1980c   "Postface." [Comment.] In *L'Impossible Prison*, pp. 316–18. [Collaborative work.] Paris: Seuil.

1980d   "Preface." *Herculine Barbin. Being the Recently Discovered Memoirs of a Nineteenth Century French Hermaphrodite.* Translated by Richard McDougall. New York: Random House.

1980e   "War in the Filigree of Peace: Course Summary." An unpublished Collège de France course summary. Translated by Ian Mcleod. *Oxford Literary Review*, 4(2):15–19.

1980f   "Table ronde du 20 mai 1978." [Discussion.] *L'Impossible Prison*, pp. 40–56. [Collaborative work.] Paris: Seuil.

1980g   "Interview. [with Millicent Dillon]." *Three Penny Review* (1980), 1(1):4–5.

1981a   "Sexuality and Solitude" [with Richard Sennett]. *London Review of Books* (21 May to 3 June 1981), 3(9):3–7.

Index

Abstractionism, in social theory, 94
Adorno, Theodor, W., 106–7; *see also*
Frankfurt School
Affective mechanisms of sexuality,
77–79, 89–91; and knowledge, as
savoir, 77–79
Althusser, Louis, xiii, 4–5, 13, 35, 110;
and Gaston Bachelard, 10; and
Georges Canguilhem, 10; and *coupure
épistémologique*, 10; and discontinuous
events, 13–14; and Foucault, 116–17;
Foucault's disagreement with, 14; and
theoretical practices, 120
Anatomy, political, 60, 75, 111
Anderson, Perry, 120
Annales historians, ix, 7, 10, 20, 44, 96,
122; their critique of *histoire
événementielle*, 11; and the Event, 12;
and events, 41–42; and Foucault's
method, 11–12; methodology of, 96;
unthought of, 13
Anthropological Sleep, 108; and Man,
23–24
Anthropologism, xiv, 67–68; in history,
108; and humanisn, 19–20; in
philosophy, 108
Anthropology: as mode of thought,
67–68; *see also* Anthropological Sleep;
Anthropologism
Archaeological method, *see* Archaeology
Archaeology: and genealogy, 57–60;
and history, 29–30; 57–60; of
knowledge, 48–56; and levels, 43–44;
as method, 42–43; and philosophy,
57–60; and politics, 57–60; and
power-knowledge, 59–60
Archaeology of Knowledge, 60; and
knowledge, 48–56; as methodological
program, 48–49; its place in
Foucault's work, 50–51; and the

statement, 51–54; its structure as a
book, 49–50
Archive: in *Archaeology of Knowledge*,
52–53; and critique, 53–54;
explained, 52–53; and history, 53–54;
and the statement, 52–53
Arendt, Hannah, xiii
Artaud, Antonin, 7, 22, 29
Author, as principle, 48

Bachelard, Gaston, 20, 44; and
Althusser, 10; and discontinuous
events, 13; and Foucault, ix, 15–18;
history of science of, 10, 15–18; vs.
Thomas S. Kuhn, 16
Barthes, Roland, xiii
Bataille, Georges, 2, 7, 21–22, 29,
65–67; and death, 25–27, 83; and
sensuality, 83; and sexuality, 25–27,
83
Bio-politics: and the body, 80–83; and
political anatomy, 80–83; *see also* Bio-
power
Bio-power, 80; and knowledge, 62; *see
also* Bio-politics
Blanchot, Maurice, 2, 20, 22, 27; and
death, 83; and writing, 83
Bloch, Marc, 98, 122
Body, x, 91; and bio-politics, 80–83; its
division, 75–76; and events, 70–71;
fractured, 70–83 *passim;* and
genealogy, 70–71; and geography,
98–99; history of, 70–83 *passim;* and
knowledge, 69–70, 81–83; and micro-
power, 69–71; as object, in field, 71;
and politics, 74, 75–76, 83–84; and
power-knowledge, 73–74; sexed, and
discipline, 81–83; its sexualization,
78–79; and soul, 75–76; space of, in
history, 70; and subjectivity, 72; time

Body (*Continued*)
of, in history, 70; and unreason, 72;
its visibility, 84
Body politic, 75–76
Book, as unit, 47
Bourdieu, Pierre, 5; his theory of
practice, 123–24
Braudel, Fernand, 96, 97, 98, 122; and
event history, 11; and Foucault,
109–10; and *la longue durée*, 10–11

Canguilhem, Georges: and Althusser,
10; and biological sciences, 15; and
discontinuous events, 13; and
Foucault, 17
Capital, theory of, 8
Center: epistemological, 67–68; and
Foucault, 8; metaphysical, 46–47; as
principle, 48
Class, 1; oppressed, 110; and power,
112; and power-knowledge, 9;
relations, and ideology, 112–14;
relations, and power, 110–11; theory
of, 112; *see also* Class analysis
Class analysis, xi; and the New Class,
117–18; and Poulantzas, 117–18; *see
also* Class
Classes: *see* Class; Class analysis
Code, disciplinary, 72–75
Communistology, 9
Comte, August, 29
Confinement, 8
Conflict, in history, 57
Conjuncture, and *Annales* historians, 11,
42–43
Connaissance: see Knowledge, as
connaissance; Connaissances
Connaissances: and discourse, 17–18; *see
also* Discipline; Disciplines; Knowledge
Coupure épistémologique, 10
Critical rationality, in social theory,
106–109
Critical theory, xiii, 119–20; and
Frankfurt School, 106–7; and history,
64–65, 109; its idealism, 122–23; *see
also* Critique; Theory
Critics, and interpreters, xii–xiii
Critique: and archive, 53–54; and
history, 53–54, 121–22; of humanism,
90; and politics, in social theory, 106;

and social theory, 27–28, 53–54,
106–9, 119–20; as theory, 64–65, 94;
and theory of power, 94; of values, by
Nietzsche, 24; *see also* Critical theory

Death, x, 91; as absence, 84; and
Bataille, 25–27, 83; and Blanchot, 83;
and Foucault, 83–84; of God, 24,
67–68; of God, in Nietzsche, 67–68,
89, 108; and history, 83–84; and
language, 21, 24–25; and life, 79–80,
118–19; as Limit, 85–86; of Man,
23–24, 67–68; and method, in social
theory, 118–24; and pathological
anatomy, 71; and politics, 83–91,
119–20; and power, 79–80; and
power-knowledge, 122–24; and
sexuality, 25–27; and subjectivity,
84–85; and transgression, 25–27,
85–86; as void, 84
Decentering: of knowledge, 47–48; of
subjectivity, 103–4; vs. relativism,
50–51
Deleuze, Gilles, 5, 22
Derrida, Jacques, 5, 46
Descent, and genealogy, 70–71
Desire, 6; and body, 76–77; history of,
102; to know, 71; and knowledge, 71,
76–78; and language, in history, 102;
and political economy, 76–77; and
power-knowledge, 76–78; and
sexuality, 71; and social relations, 62;
and subjectivity, 104–5; and will to
power, 90–91; and will to truth, 63
Discipline, 34; as code, 72–75; and
knowledge, as *savoir,* 72–75; meanings
of, 19–20; and semiotechniques,
72–75; and the sexed body, 81–83;
social, 71; *see also* Disciplines
Disciplines: as *connaissances,* 36; and
power-knowledge, 88–89; and
practices, 19–20; *see also* Discipline
Discontinuities: and events, 13; in
history, 15–17, 41–42, 100–1
Discourse, 21–22, 91; and the
disciplines, 17–18; ellipsis of, 60–63;
as field, 54–56; as formation, 53–55;
in Foucault's method, 38–39; and
history, 59–60, 61, 96; and
knowledge, 6, 47–48, 60–63; and

politics, 119–20; and power-knowledge, 40–41, 76–78; as practice, 33–37; as practice, and documents, 37–38; and practices, 33–37, 38–39, 48, 61; of sexuality, and power, 79–80; on sexuality, and power-knowledge, 76–78; and social relations, 54–55, 97, 99–100; and social formations, 54–55, 97, 99–100; as relations, 55; and rules, 38–39; and theory, 86–88; and transgressive history, 96–97; *see also* Discursive formations; Discursive relations

Discursive formations, 53–54, 61–62, 96–97; as field, 54–56; and knowledge, 61–63; and power-knowledge, 61–63, 98; and series, in history, 54; vs. social formations, 54–55; and statements, 61–62, 96–97; *see also* Discursive relations; Formations; Relations

Discursive relations, 55; and social institutions, 99–100; vs. social relations, 61–62, 97, 99–100; *see also* Discursive formations; Formations; Relations

Dispersion, 15; of events, 43–44

Dispositif de sexualité; see Affective mechanisms of sexuality; Sexuality

Documentation, avoided, as style, 32

Documents, 46; and discursive practices, 37–38; in history, 11, 37–38, 100–1, 121–22; in history, and discourse, 96; and knowledge, 55–56; and monuments, 100–1; and practices, 37–38

Durkheim, Emile, 29

Economism, 9

Empiricism, 33; in history, 45; and rationalism, 120–1

Ennoncé, le, see Statement

Epistemology: categories of, transgressed, 96; as center, 67–68

Epistemological break, *see Coupure épistémologique*

Epistemological thresholds, 17–19

Epistemologization, threshold of, 18

Eroticism, and sexuality, 26–27

Error, in history, 15–17

Eternal Return, and transgression, 65

Ethnomethodology, xiii

Event, the: and *Annales* historians, 12; and Foucault, 3–7; and *histoire événementielle*, 3–4; *see also,* Events

Event History, 11; *see also Histoire événementielle*

Events: and *Annales* historians, 41–42; and the body, 70; dispersed, 43–44; great, and *historie événementielle*, 3–4; and history, 3–4, 11, 42–43, 96; in history, their positivity; inscribed on the body, 70; and Nietzsche, 41–42; and practices, 33–37; as reversals in history, 43–44; series of, in history, 36–37; their singularity, 97; and structures, 12; *see also* Event

Exceptional case, and style, 30–32

Excess: and the Limit, 68–70; and transgression, 68–70

Existentialism, and structuralism, 4

Fact, and knowledge, 44–48, 58

Febvre, Lucien, 97

Field: discursive, 54–56; discursive, and knowledge, 55–56; of objectivity, and the body, 71; political, and the body, 74; and regularities, 52–54, 54–56

Finitude: and knowledge, 67–68; Man's 67–68

Formalism, 17–18, 46; in history, 14, 59; in history, and practices, 33; and social theory, 93, 94, 120

Formalization, 17–18

Formations: social, 54; *see also* Discursive formations; Discursive relations; Relations

Foucault, Michel: and Althusser, 14, 116–17; his ambiguity about power-knowledge, 58–59; and *Annales* historians, ix; and Bachelard, ix, 15–18; background, question of, ix; biographic facts, vii; and Braudel, 109–10; and Canguilhem, 17; and discourse, 38–39; and Event, 3–7; and historicism, 21; how to read, 91; and Lacan, 109–10; and language, 20–28; his limits, 109–10; and Marxism, ix, 7–10; his method, 7–14, 32–44 *passim*, 120–21; and naturalism, 108, 119;

Foucault, Michel (*Continued*)
  and Nietzsche, ix; and Paris, 2–3; and
  phenomenology, xi, 21; politics of, x;
  and positivism, xi, 21; and post-
  structuralism, 5–7; questions of, 95; as
  semiotician, ix; and social theory, xi,
  110–25 *passim*; and structuralism, ix,
  4–5, 7, 21; style of, ix; theory of
  capital, 8
Frankfurt School, 96; and critical
  theory, 106–7; and subjectivity, 106–8
Freedom: and Frankfurt School, 107;
  and subjectivity, 107
Freud, Sigmund, 7; and post-
  structuralism, 6

Garfinkel, Harold, 123
Genealogy, and archaeology, 57–60; and
  body, 70–71; and emergence, 70–71;
  and events, 70–71; and history,
  57–60, 70–71; Nietzsche's idea of, 44;
  and philosophy, 57–60; and politics,
  57–60
Geography, and the body, 98
Giddens, Anthony, 110, 114, 123–24
God: death of, 67–68; death of, and
  Nietzsche, 108
Gouldner, Alvin W., xiii, 110, 114, 118;
  and the New Class, 118
Guattari, Felix, 5

Habermas, Juergen, 96, 106–7; and
  practical norms, 116; and the State,
  115; and teleology, 123; *see also*
  Frankfurt School; Critical theory
Hegel, Friedrich, 35
Hermeneutics, 94; and pure theory,
  122–23
Histoire événementielle, 11, 12; and
  Annales historians, 11, critique of, 11;
  and events, 3–4; and great events,
  3–4; *see also* Event history
Historicism, 21, 94
History: and anthropologism, 108; and
  archaeology, 29, 57–60; and archive,
  53–54; of body, 70–83 *passim;* changes
  in, 43–44; as conflict, 39–40, 43–44,
  57; and critical theory, 64–65, 109;
  and critique, 53–54, 121–22; and
  death, 83–84; and discontinuities,

41–42, 100–1; and discourse, 59–61,
  96; documents in, 11, 37–38, 96,
  100–1; and empiricism, 45; and error,
  15–17; and events, 11, 42–43, 96; and
  formalism, 14, 33; and genealogy,
  57–60; 70–71; historizing, 96; and
  idealism, 14, 45–46, 70; and
  immanent truth, 65; interpretivist,
  and practices, 33; and knowledge,
  14–20, 59–60; 89–90; and knowledge,
  as *connaissance*, 59–60; and linearity,
  14, 41–42; of the long term, 36; and
  materialism; 15–18; method of, ix–x,
  36–37; and monuments, 11, 100–1;
  and philosophy, 57–60; and
  pluralism, 15–17; and politics, 13–14,
  57–60, 86–88, 96; and positivism, 14,
  33, 96, 97; and power-knowledge,
  59–60, 84–85; and practices, 61; as
  reconstruction 37, 59–60; and
  revolutionary will to power, 94–95;
  reversals in, 43–44; and ruptures, 10,
  41–42; and social theory, 53–54; and
  structures, 100–1; as struggle, 36,
  39–40; totalizing, 14, 96, 98;
  traditional, xi, 3, 96; and
  transcendental truth, 65;
  transformations in, 100–1; and
  transgression, 69–70, 89–90;
  transgression of, 93; transgressive,
  and discourse, 96–97; and truth, 65;
  and truth, as risk, 124–25; and the
  unthought, 10; and visibility, 46; and
  will to power, 94–95
Hobsbawn, Eric J., 122
Homocentrism, 19; *see also*
  Anthropology; Anthropologism
Horkheimer, Max, 106–7; *see also*
  Frankfurt School
Humanism: critique of, 90; and
  liberalism, 19–20
Human sciences, 57

Idealism, 101; in critical theory, 122–23;
  in history, 14, 45–46, 70; and social
  theory, 93, 94, and subjectivity, 107
Ideal speech situation, 107
Ideas, in history, 70
Identity, concept of, 107

Ideology, xiv; and class relations, 112–14; end of, debate over, 118; and science, 113–14; and social theory, 94; and truth, 112–14
Inscription, of power-knowledge, and the body, 73–74
Intellectuals: bourgeois, 87; concrete, 87–88; concrete, and discursive practices, 106; concrete, and the New Class, 118; and the New Class, 117–18; and Paris, 2–3; and politics, 86–88; and practice of knowledge, 87–88; theory of, xiv; and *tout Paris*, 3; universal, 87–88
Intelligibility, of practices, 35–37
Interpretation, and style, xi–xv
Interpreters, and critics, xii–xiii
Interpretivism, in history, and practices, 33
Invisibility: of social field, 46; *see also* Visibility

Jakobson, Roman, 5
Jarry, Alfred, 29

Kant, Immanuel, and Man, 18–19
Klossowski, Pierre, 22
Knowledge: archaeology of, 48–56 *passim;* and *Archaeology of Knowledge,* 48–56 *passim;* and the body, 69–70; and bio-politics of the body, 81–83; as *connaissance,* 48, 59–60, 61; as *connaissance,* and discursive formations, 61–63; as *connaissance,* epistemic, 61; as *connaissance,* vs. as *savoir,* 59–60; decentered, 47–48; and desire, 71; discontinuities in history of, 16–17; and discourse, 6, 47–48, 60–63; and documents, 55–56; epistemic, 48; excluded, 38–39; and fact, 44–48, 58; and finitude, 67–68; history of, 14–20; and Man, 67–68; and micro-power, 69–71; as plural, 16; and power, 27, 34–35, 56; as *savoir,* 36, 48; as *savoir,* accumulated, 61; as *savoir,* and affective mechanisms of sexuality, 77–79; as *savoir,* and the body, 72–75; as *savoir,* vs. as *connaissance,* 59–60, 61; as *savoir,* and discipline, 72–75; as *savoir,* and

discursive formations, 61–63; as *savoir,* in history, 59–60; as *savoir,* and power, 113–14; and sexuality, 62, 77–79; as subject of *Archaeology of Knowledge,* 48–50, 55–56; transgressive, 67–69
Kristeva, Julia, 96; her concept of praxis, 103–4; and subjectivity, 103–5
Kuhn, Thomas S., 20; vs. Bachelard, 15–17

Labor, and semiotics, 103–4
Labor power, 74
Lacan, Jacques, 96; and Foucault, 109–10; and the Other, 102; and post-structuralism, 6; and subjectivity, 101–2, 104, 105
Ladurie, Emmanuel Le Roy, *see* Le Roy Ladurie, Emmanuel
Language: and death, 21, 24–25; and death of Man, 24–25; and desire in history, 102; in Foucault, 20–28; and the Limit, 66–68; and power-knowledge, 84–85; and social theory, 94–95; and the Subject, 66–67; and transgression, 26–28; of transgression, 65–68; and will to power, 24–25
Lecourt, Dominique, 44
Lefebvre, Georges, 98
Le Roy Ladurie, Emmanuel, 12, 98
Lévi-Strauss, Claude, 4, 5, 20–21, 29
Liberal Age, 8, 12; as episteme, 19–20; and Man, 19–20; *see also* Liberalism
Liberalism: and humanism, 19–20; and Man, 27; *see also* Liberal Age
Libido sciendi: and taboo, 62; and transgression of modesty, 71; *see also* Will to know
Life: and death, 79–80, 118–119; and power, 79–80; and power-knowledge, 122
Limit, the: death as, 85–86; and excess, 68–70; Foucault's, 109–10; and language, 66–68; and transgression, 66–67, 68–70, 84–85
Linearity: in history, 14, 41–42; and time, in history, 96
Longue durée, la, 10–14 *passim;* and structures, 45–46

Magritte, René, 4
Mallarmé, Stéphane, 22
Man, 21; and anthropological sleep,
   23–24; and death, 23–25; death of,
   67–68; disappearance of, and
   subjectivity, 106; and finitude, 67–68;
   and God, 24; and Kant, 18–19, and
   knowledge, 18–19, 67–68; knowledge
   of, 18–20; in Liberal Age, 19–20, 27;
   and power, 27; and sexuality, 25–27;
   theory of, xiv
Marcuse, Herbert, xiii
Marx, Karl, 7, 20, 29, 118; capital,
   theory of, 8; and Foucault, 13–14;
   and method, 122
Marxism, 1, 35, 44; and Foucault, ix, xi,
   7–10 passim; scientific, 114; unthought
   of, 12
Materialism: and discourse, 100; and
   discursive practices, 62–63; and
   history, 15–18; and social theory, 93,
   94
Merleau-Ponty, Maurice, 70, 105
Metaphysics: classical, and subjectivity,
   104–5; idealist, 107
Method: and death, in social theory,
   118–124; Foucault's, 32–44 passim,
   120–21; historical, 30; Marx's, 122;
   and practices, 33, 35–38; and rules,
   32–35; in social theory, and power-
   knowledge, 121–22; and style, 30–32
Methodology: Foucault's contribution to,
   121–22; see also Methods
Micro-power: and the body, 69–71; and
   the disciplines, 69–71; and
   knowledge, 69–71
Miliband, Ralph, 110, 114
Monuments: and documents, 100–1; in
   history, 11, 100–1, 121–22

Naturalism: and Foucault, 108, 119; and
   Habermas, 119; and Lévi-Strauss,
   119; in social theory, 119
New Class: and intellectuals, 117–18;
   and Ruling Class, 117–18; and Alain
   Touraine, 118
Nietzsche, Fredrich, 2, 6, 7, 19, 20, 22,
   29, 70–71; and death of God, 89; and
   the Event, in history, 41–42; and
   Foucault, as shifter, 22–23; and

Freud, 23–24; and genealogy, 44; and
   genealogy, as descent, 7–71; and
   genealogy, as emergence, 70–71; and
   Marx, 23–24; and the Overman, 89,
   108; and politics, 122; and Return of
   the Same, 108; and sociology, 24–25;
   and will to power, 24–25
Norms, practical, and State control, 115
Objectivism, 123–24; in structuralism,
   50
Objectivity, 94, 101; and power-
   knowledge, 84–85
O'Connor, James, 110
Oeuvre, as unit, 47
Offe, Claus, 110, 114; and the State,
   115
Oppositive structure, as style, 30–32
Origin: and experience, 63; as principle,
   48
Other, the, and Lacan, 102
Overman: concept of, 108; and
   Nietzsche, 89

Parkin, Frank, 110, 117
Paris: and Foucault, 2–3; and
   intellectuals, 2–3
Parsons, Talcott, xiii
Phenomenology, xiii; and Foucault, xi,
   21; as subjectivism, 123
Philosophy: and anthropologism, 108;
   and archaeology, 57–60; and
   genealogy, 57–60; and history, 57–60;
   and politics, 57–60; transgression of,
   93
Pluralism, and history, 15–17
Political anatomy, 60, 111; and bio-
   politics, 80–83; of body, and desire,
   76–77; see also Political economy;
   Politics
Political economy, 60; of desire, 76–77;
   and the State, 111–12; see also Political
   anatomy; Politics
Politics: as action, and knowledge, 114;
   and archaeology, 57–60; and the
   body, 75–76, 83–84; and death,
   83–91, 119–20; and discourse,
   119–20; and economics, 60; and
   genealogy, 57–60; and history, 13–14,
   57–60, 86–88, 96, 98–99; and
   intellectuals, 86–88; and Nietzsche,

122; and philosophy, 57–60; and political anatomy, 75; and power-knowledge, 84–85; as practice, 124; transgression of, 93; *see also* Political anatomy; Political economy

Positivism: and Foucault, xi, 21; in history, 14, 33, 96, 97; and practices, 33

Positivity: of historical events, 97; of power, 88–89; threshold of, 17

Post-structuralism: and Foucault, 7; and Freud, 6; and Lacan, 6; and Marx, 6; and the Subject, 6

Poulantzas, Nicos, xiii, 4, 110, 114; and class analysis, 117–18

Power: and class analysis, 112; and critique, 94; and death, 79–80; and desire, 90–91; and determinism, 6; and discourse of sexuality, 79–80; as immanent, 6; and knowledge, 27, 34–35; 56; and knowledge, as *savoir*, 113–14; labor, 74; and life, 79–80; machinery of, 10; and Man, 77; and micro-power, 69–71; its positivity, 88–89; relations of, 110–11; relations of, and social relations, 111–12; relations of, and the State, 111–12, 114–15; and social theory, 58–59, 110–18; sovereign, 73; state, and Skocpol, 115–16; and statements, 97; theory of, xiv, 6, 94; and truth, 88; will to, 24–25, 90–91; and will to truth, 63, 88

Power-knowledge, 56, 58–60, 69–70; and archaeology, 59–60; and class, 9–10; and conflict, in history, 43–44; and death, 122–24; and desire, 76–78; and the disciplines, 88–89; and discourse, 40–41, 76–78, 98; and discursive formations, 61–63, 98; as epistemic strategy, 98; as field of concepts, 76–77; and historical change, 43–44; and history, 43–44, 84–85; inscribed on body, 73–74; and language, 84–85; and life, 122; local centers of, 42; and methodology, 121–22; and objectivity, 84–85; and politics, 84–85; and practice, 34–35, 39–41, 120–21; and reconstruction in history, 121–22; and revolutionary

action, 91; and rules, 39–41; and the State, 111–12, 116–17; and struggle in history, 43–44; and theory, 120–21; and transgression, 26–27, 64–66, 84–85; as unique concept, x; and violence, 63–66; and visibility of practices, 39–41; and will to truth, 63–66; *see also* Power

Practice: of knowledge, and intellectuals, 98; and power-knowledge, 120–21; and theory, 86–88, 120–21 *see also* Practices; Praxis

Practices: and the disciplines, 19–20; and discourse, 38–39, 61; discursive, 33–37, 49, 61; discursive, and concrete intellectuals, 106; discursive, and materiality, 62–63; and events, 33–37; and history, 61; and intellectuals, 87–88; intelligibility of, 35–37; and method, 33, 35–38; and politics, 124; and power-knowledge, 34–35, 39–41; regulated, 34; and reversals, 43–44; theory of, Bourdieu's, 123; visibility of, 35–37; *see also* Practice; Praxis

Pragmatism, American, 123

Praxis: Kristeva's concept of, 103–4; semiotic, 103–4; and subjectivity, 104; *see also* Practice; Practices

Rationalism, and empiricism, 120–21

Rationality; critical, in social theory, 106–9; as practice, 116

Reason: normative, 107; and unreason, 49

Reconstruction: in history, 37, 38, 46, 59–60; in history, and power-knowledge, 121–23

Regle, la, see Rules

Regularité, la, see Regularities

Regularities: as field, 52–54, 54–56; and practices, 34; and rules, 54–56

Relations: *see* Discursive relations; Formations; Social Relations; Power

Relativism, 47; and decentering, 50–51

Return of the Same, 108

Revolutionary action, and power-knowledge, 91

Roussel, Raymond, 20, 22

Rules: and discourse, 38–39; and

Rules (*Continued*)
method, 32–35; and power-
knowledge, 39–41; and regularities,
54–56
Ruling Class, and the New Class,
117–18
Ruptures, 15; in history, 41–42; history
of, 10–11

Sade, Donatien Alphonse François,
Marquis de, 20, 22
Sartre, Jean Paul, xiii, 104
Saussure, Ferdinand de, 5, 20
Savoir, see Knowledge, as *savoir*
Science: Bachelard's history of, 10, 15;
and ideology, 113–14; philosophy of,
xiv; pure, 94; and the unthought, 18;
see also Sciences
Sciences: human, 18–20; *see also* Science
Semiology, *see* Semiotics
Semiotechnique, 72, *see also* Semiotics
Semiotics, xiii, 1, 62; and Foucault, ix;
and history, 99; as practice, 103–4; as
semiotechnique, 69; and structuralism,
21; as system, and labor, 103–4; as
technique, 72–75
Sensuality: and Bataille, 83; *see also*
Sexuality
Series: and discursive formations,
54–55; in historical method, 36–37
Serres, Michel, 13
Sexuality, 34; affective mechanisms of,
77–79, 89–91; and Bataille, 25–27;
and bodies; 89–90; and death, 25–27;
discourse of, and power, 79–80;
discourse on, and power-knowledge,
76–78; and eroticism, 26–27; and
knowledge, as *savoir*, 77–78; and Man,
25–27; and pleasure, 89
Sign, absolute, 23
Silence, and transgression, 124–25
Skocpol, Theda, 110, 114, 115–16; and
State power, 115–16
Social formations, *see* Formations
Social relations: of capitalism, 99; and
discourse, 61–62, 97, 99–100; vs.
discursive, 61–62, 97, 99–100; and
domination, 62; and power, 111–12;
their visibility, 99; *see also* Formations;
Relations

Social theory: and abstractionism, 94;
critical, 64–65; and critique, 106,
119–20; and critique, in politics, 106;
as critique, 53–54, 119–20; and death,
118–24; defined, 93–94; and
discourse, 99–100; and formalism, 93,
94; and Foucault, xi, 93–96, 96–125
passim; and history, 53–4; and
ideology, 94; and methods, 118–24;
and politics, 106; and power, 110–18;
and social relations, 99–100; and time,
96–100; and transgression, 3, 27–28,
120–24, 124–25; *see also* Theory
Sociology, political, 116
Soul, and body, 75–76
Space, and time, 97–98, 100
State: apparatus, 111–12; control, and
practical norms, 115; and Habermas,
115; and Offe, 115; power, and
Skocpol, 115–16; and power-
knowledge, 111–12, 116–17; and
power relations, 111–12; relative
autonomy of, and power, 114–15
Statement, the: in *Archaeology of
Knowledge*, 51–54; and the archive,
52–53; as concept, 52–53; *see also*
Statements
Statements: and discursive formations,
61–62, 96; and linguistics, 51–52; and
power, 97; and power-knowledge,
61–63
Structuralism, xiii, 1; and existentialism,
4; and Foucault, ix, 4–5, 7, 21; its
objectivism, 50; as semiotics, 21
Structures, in history, 45–46, 100–1
Style: and documentation, 32; and
exceptional case, 30–31; and
interpretation, xi–xv; and method,
30–32; and oppositive structure,
31–32
Subject: founding, 63; and language,
66; and post-structuralism, 6;
transcendental, 27; *see also* Subjectivity
Subjectivity: and the body, 72; and
classical metaphysics, 104–5; critique
of, 100; and death, 84–85; and
decentering, 103–4; and desire,
104–5; elimination of, in history, 101;
and Frankfurt School, 106–8; and
freedom, 107; founding, 100; and

Man, 105; and originary experience, 100; as phenomenology, 123; and signification, 103–4; and social practices, 104; and social theory, 100–6; transcendental, 6; *see also* Subject

Taboo: and transgression, 26, 28; and violence, 64–66
Tel Quel, and subjectivity, 101
Tertiary spatializations, 61
Theory: critical, 106–9; and critique, 94; and discourse, 86–88, 99–100; and power-knowledge, 120–21; and practice, 86–88, 120–21; pure, and hermeneutics, 122–23; *see also* Social theory
Thompson, E. P., 122
Thought, anthropological, 67–68
Thresholds, epistemological, 17–19
Time: Foucault's conception of, critique, 96–100; as linear, 96; and social theory, 96–100; and space, 97–98, 100; spatialized, 11
Touraine, Alain: and historicity, 123–24; and the New Class, 118
Tout Paris, and intellectuals, 3
Transformation, in history, 100–1
Transgression, x, 63–70; and death, 26–28, 85–86; of epistemological categories, 96; and Eternal Return, 65; and excess, 68–70; and history, 69–70, 89–90, 93, 96–97; in history, and discourse, 96–97; of history, 83; and knowledge, 67–9; as knowledge, and history, 89–90; and language, 26–28, 65–68; and *libido sciendi,* 71; and the Limit, 66–68, 68–70; of

limits, 84–85; of philosophy, 93; of politics, 93; and power-knowledge, 26–27, 63–66, 84–85; and silence, 124–25; and social theory, 3, 27–28, 120–25; and taboo, 26, 28; three types of, 63, 65; and truth, 65; and will to know, 71; and will to truth, 63–66
Truth: and Eternal Return, 65; and history, 65, 124–25; ideal, 65; and ideology, 112–13; and power, 88; and transgression, 65; will to, 63, 64; *see also* Will to truth; Will to know

Universal pragmatics of communication, 107
Unthought: of *Annales* historians, 13; and history, 10; in Marxism, 10, 12; and science, 18

Violence: and power-knowledge, 63–66; and taboo, 63–66; and transgression, 64–66, 69–70
Visibility, 49; of the body, 84; in history, 46; of practices, 35–37; of practices, and power-knowledge, 39–41; of social relations, 99

Wallerstein, Immanuel, 110, 122, 124
Will to know, 60; and taboo, 62; *see also* Will to truth
Will to power: and desire, 90–91; and history, 94–95; revolutionary, 94–95
Will to truth, 63; and desire, 63; and power, 63; and power-knowledge, 63–66; and transgression 63; and violence, 63–66; *see also* Will to know
Writing: Blanchot's view of, 83